Scribbling Sisters

D1293131

Scribbling Sisters

Dale & Lynne Spender

University of Oklahoma Press
Norman and London

For Mum

Library of Congress Cataloging-in-Publication Data

Spender, Dale.
    Scribbling sisters.

    Reprint. Originally published : London, England :
Camden Press, c1986.
    1. Spender, Dale--Correspondence. 2. Spender,
Lynne--Correspondence. 3. Women--Australia--
Correspondence. I. Spender, Lynne. II. Title.
CT2808.S67A4 1987   994.06'3'0922   87-40217
ISBN 0-8061-2096-7

Published in the U.S.A. under
license from Camden Press Ltd,
43 Camden Passage, London N1 8EB, England,
by the University of Oklahoma Press,
Norman, Publishing Division of the University.
Copyright © Dale Spender, Lynne Spender.
No part of this book may be reproduced in any form
without permission from Camden Press Ltd. except for the
quotation of brief passages in criticism.
First printing of the
University of Oklahoma Press edition, 1987.

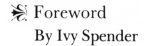 Foreword
By Ivy Spender

When my second daughter Lynne was born almost three years after her sister, I was delighted. Not having a sister myself I daydreamed about each of them having a constant companion through life, always able to enjoy things together. In their early years there were times when there was little togetherness but let any other person criticise or oppose either one in any way and they became as inseparable as Siamese Twins.

As they grew up my dreams were realised; they were and are, each to the other, best friend, chief adviser and ever present helper even when living thousands of miles apart.

There were times in their late teens when I had difficulty assimilating some of their progressive ideas: I learnt later, but not too late, to compromise, to encourage them to support and monitor each other's actions so that the necessity for me to 'interfere' was removed.

Believing always that one's children are only lent to one for a short period I hoped to make that period a little longer by helping them whenever possible, both emotionally and materially; always with 'no strings attached' – loose ties but no knots.

In December 1977 I travelled to Brisbane to see Lynne; a disappointed Lynne after the birth of her second son; she had so wanted a daughter. The comfort I offered was that she didn't need a daughter – as I had needed a daughter in the absence of a sister; she had Dale.

Over the years as they and I have pursued our own paths we have found ourselves separated by great distances with letters forming the contact lines; we have written to each other of our plans, problems, hopes, achievements, disappointments and successes, as well as our day to day happenings. Our letters have been a strong life-line stretched half way round the world; to me they are a continuous message of love and dependence – to each of them a sounding board for their whole living. And it is from some of their letters that this book has evolved.

A source of continual happiness in my life has been the supporting love and protection existing between my dearly loved daughters. I am proud to be their mother.

The greatest gift I have given them is each to the other.

Ivy Spender,
Milton Hospital,
January 1983

✣ Introduction:
A personal view of the facts

We like writing to each other. We know it takes time, but probably not as much time as we would spend in each other's company – 'just talking' – as we would undoubtedly spend if we were both living in the same city. Of course it isn't 'just talking'; it's the bricks and mortar of our relationship and we both know it is no hardship to do something which makes you feel good. And we do feel very good about each other, and we get enormous pleasure from the letters.

Part of the pleasure is receiving them. We each arrange our own days around the possibility of a letter – in much the same way as arrangements are made to meet a friend. A time, a place, an 'occasion' has to be set up. Our letters to each other need space; they can't be read on the way to the bus stop or while preparing the children's breakfast. They demand, minimally, a quarter of an hour, (preferably child free) and a cup of coffee or a glass of wine, not to mention a generous amount of physical space . . . to put your feet up.

This is because they are not just inventories of where we have been or how much it costs, but are our conversations with each other. We really do try and maintain in our (almost) daily letters, the same links we had when we lived under the same roof. We do try to exchange the insights and understandings about the world . . . as well as the personal detail . . . that we swapped so readily when face-to-face.

But another part of the pleasure is the writing. Both of us enjoy writing and in some ways our daily letter writing is a practice, an apprenticeship. While the blank white page in the typewriter may be threatening when contracted for a publisher, it holds no fears when it is seen as a page of a letter to a sister. Those mornings when it may be easier to do anything *but* write the next chapter of the book which is already overdue, there seems to be little difficulty in writing a letter; and in the process of relating what the problem is (why you feel nauseous about writing, or why the chapter won't come together), the problem generally recedes even if it does not completely disappear. For both of us our public writing has often been generated and clarified through our private writing and in our letters are the skeletal outlines of many chapters and books – as well as the discarded remnants of what we think it better not to write. Some people keep diaries to organise their thoughts for themselves . . . we write diaries for each other.

Undeniably this leads to complications. It is not just that we must get out 'the letters' when we want to do our public writing (and we each keep a carbon copy so we each have a 'full set'), but when we *are* together, we can find ourselves in the peculiar position at times of having to consult the letters. We sit and talk and look up what we wrote, so that the written dialogue becomes enmeshed with the spoken dialogue. (We have not – as yet – when together, resorted to letter writing to each other from different rooms of the house . . . but that is basically because we have resisted the temptation!) Both of us are firm believers in the principle that we don't know what we think until we see what we write – and it is a principle that can still apply even after we have talked all day.

Letter writing also has the advantage of widening the horizon. It is possible to take many more 'risks', to be much more speculative when writing to each other than it is when writing for a public audience. This is partly because there is no requirement that our writing conform to the established standards of the 'finished product'. It doesn't matter if our sentences are ungrammatical, if our ideas are hazy or crazy. We don't have to maintain the same degree of 'control', with the result that the process of writing, of thinking and organising ideas, is much more obvious.

We can do this because we have no fear of each other as the audience. We are not 'judges' and we do not need to worry about libel laws or academic reputations. We are not going to take each other to court, or recommend psychiatric care . . . or even reject each other.

So our letter-writing is not for us a substitute . . . it is a bonus. The space to speculate – and to refine – is rare; the room to contemplate, to reflect, to revise is not readily available to many (and certainly isn't fostered by our education system). Writing to each other, we not only have quick and encouraging feedback, a luxury few writers can arrange, we also provide each other with penalty-free-permission to give vent to our rage, to record our emotional routes, to write freely and to ask . . . What if women were in charge of the world?

As assertive feminists it is understandable that we should be somewhat preoccupied with this question – what would be the shape of society if women were in charge? (Only half the time, of course – we are not greedy!) And it was during one of our discussions about what would change that we first thought of publishing some of our letters. Surrounded by appallingly typed letters, and after a day of much talk – and even more wine – in Sydney, April 1982, we were lamenting the fact that women had never been more than twenty percent of the published authors – despite the considerable evidence that women have written (and read) more than men.*

Women have predominantly been the letter writers, the diary keepers, the journal jotters and it is no accident that women do usually enjoy low status. So although women have this vast *literature*, it has rarely been considered *literary* by those in charge, and so much of women's writing remains as Virginia Woolf stated in 1929 in 'Women and Fiction', 'stuffed away in old drawers' (p.141).

Yet this is not just because of the form of the writing as some

---

* This is the substance of Lynne's book '*Intruders on the Rights of Man: Women's Unpublished Heritage*', Pandora Press, 1983.

men of letters have suggested. When the letters, diary or journal of a woman are published or republished today (generally by a feminist press), there is no lack of interest in them – at least not by women. And the form of the diary has never been an obstacle to men's literary reputations: on the contrary, the diaries of Pepys or Boswell (as well as the diaries of many prominent male politicians too numerous to name) have been accorded a literary and authoritative status unknown to females. So it isn't the form, or the writing, which has excluded women's letters and diaries from the publishers' lists. It's the sex!

Well, that's a challenge, isn't it?

(It's certainly something that would change if women were in charge.) It's a challenge though on more than one front. As feminists we both feel very strongly about the value of the *process* in contrast to the 'finished product'. We like knowing *how* people come to hold their beliefs and opinions, and we want to know the paths they took to arrive at their present positions. We do not feel the necessity to sift the 'intellectual' from the 'emotional' for to us, the way we look at the world and make sense of it, depends as much on our emotions as our intellect. And yet the model of non-fiction writing which is usually held up as desirable is one in which feeling and thinking are ostensibly rigorously separated.

The split between 'reason' and 'emotion' which characterises our male-dominated society is not one which we subscribe to for we not only think it false, we think it destructive. And it is a split which women have been able to avoid through writing, especially through the writing of letters and diaries. For are not these but a *personal view of the facts?* And yet there is really no category for this 'aberration'. Letters and diaries do fall into that realm between the personal and the factual, between fiction and non-fiction, and while this may be sufficient evidence for some to ignore such writing, for us it is just another reason for challenging the categories.

And besides, we feel another challenge. Having become tired of having many of our publicly expressed ideas dismissed as personal and polemical, we thought it would make a pleasant change to have our privately expressed feelings dismissed as political.

But there has been a world of difference between our defiant decision to publish (and be damned) and the preparation of this manuscript. While the substance of this book *is* our letters as they were written, we have had to make changes – for many reasons.

First of all when we met up again in December 1982, each with our bundle of 'the letters' under our arm, we soon realised we would have to do some severe editing. We had all our letters from April onwards . . . and we just had far too many. More like enough for ten books than one. Being very logical women we started at the beginning but this meant that we stopped in August . . . for no better reason than that we had the required number of pages. We also found that bits and pieces of 'topics' were scattered throughout different letters and that it would probably be easier for the reader if we put them together. So there was a considerable amount of 'cut and paste' activity and there is now only one letter, for example, on the Falklands war instead of many references in many letters.

Obviously we had a substantial editing task when we came to consider the laws of libel. When the law makes it clear that the issue is not whether a statement is true but whether it takes away a man's 'good' name we found much to excise; in our letters we quite intentionally at times seek to show the false nature of many a 'good' man's reputation, and so regrettably, some of that writing had to go. And of course we had to remove any references that those who knew us might have found hurtful. Some of our 'nasty' bits therefore have been removed, but where they are unlikely to harm anyone, some do remain.

Apart from that, it is pretty much 'warts and all'; the ungrammatical sentences, the hazy, crazy ideas, the highs and the lows. We both agree that without the other we would not have the nerve to go through with this. We both realise we are made extremely vulnerable by bringing some of our private life to public view, by trying to make the personal political – but we have decided that not only will we cry on each other's shoulder if we are damned – but really, that it won't be so terribly new and we can always write to each other about it!

And we are both convinced – on at least two days out of three anyway – that we are trying to show feminism as a process, a personal/political reality, and not just as a public position. We are both convinced (three days out of three) that many women communicate in the way that we do but that it remains invisible in a male-dominated world. We think it is time to come out.

We also have our mother to fall back on – although at the time we were putting these letters together that was hardly an appropriate term. We had thought that it might be difficult to persuade her to sanction this venture (she is still protective despite our years) and to write the Foreword. But the real difficulty was when she broke her pelvis – water skiing – and ceased to be available for child care! Perhaps we took advantage of her handicapped state – we insisted that she write in hospital. And we both cried when we read what she had written.

But the book was completed, mother began to heal, and we, and the children, survived. We continue to write to each other in much the same form as our letters are reproduced here. And we continue to chant daily – to invoke the protection of the goddess and to ward off the wrath of the gods – that the distinction between the public and the private has served male ends, and that the personal is political.

⚹ Background

Dale lives with Ted Brown in Chelsea, London; Lynne lives with her sons Jay and Aaron (who were 7 and 4 respectively at the time of writing) in Coogee. Dale and Lynne have a younger brother Graeme, who lives with Penny, and 'Mum' and 'Dad' are Ivy and Harry Spender, who live in Wollongong. Karen is Lynne's Monday to Friday lodger and there is an assortment of friends throughout the letters – Sue, Ruth, Jill, Robyn, Lizzie, Pippa, Renate, Anna.

Dale returned from Sydney to London in April 1982 when the Falkland War was in progress and when these letters commence.

Dear Lou,*

Back in the land of the raised eyebrow again – and I am not all that sure that I can read the code completely. The immigration man raised his left eyebrow – and let me through; the customs man raised his left eyebrow – and stopped me. It's all very well for the English to rely on left eyebrows while we lesser mortals are confined to words (or more explicit gestures) but I do wish they would issue some sort of dictionary of usage for us, to avoid confusion. I'm still convinced that the English feel the same range of emotions as any other cultural group, it's just that they have developed their own tricky style of expression. To this day I don't know whether it means 'go to the top of the class' or 'never waste my time again' when eminent male professors inform me in expressionless tones that my work is 'very interesting'. (I'd be a bit of a dunce if I couldn't work out which meaning was more likely though!)

Was it Australian defensiveness which prompted all those questions about the possibility – and indeed the probability – of Australian males being the worst in the world? The goddess forbid that I should ever be caught making a case for the defence of the Australian boy but I can't see that he is much different

---

* Lou is the family name for Lynne – from Lindy Lou.

from his English counterpart; it seems to me that while one uses words (and gestures) to make his point, the other resorts to the left eyebrow. And in the sum total of human affairs, I don't think that qualifies as progress – although I have to admit it's somewhat easier on the ears.

The trip back was pretty much routine . . . the usual awful air travel. I really do think that the way airlines treat passengers contravenes the charter of human rights. They lock you up, confine you to a small space, completely restrict your movements, provide no bathing amenities and inadequate toilet facilities, keep you awake with lights and flickering movements on a screen, and feed you at irregular intervals with plastic food (not to mention the coffee which is obviously designed to damage even the most robust digestive system). It would be illegal anywhere on the ground. Is it that the laws of the land don't apply in the air? Maybe you could take this as the burning question which forces you to do a law degree in order to find out the answer; any selection committee would be bound to be impressed by your determination to uphold the standards of the legal profession and would admit you immediately.

I was pretty tired when I got to Heathrow and was almost ready to resolve that I would never eat, drink, or smoke again with such gay abandon the night before the 'down under' or 'up over' trip. But then I remembered the bottle of wine we had at the airport and decided that it was the wine before ascension which was the cause of all evil. So I just resolved that in future I would not *finish* the bottle before departure; do you think I will notice an improvement?

After thirty six hours of travelling I was not in the best frame of mind when it came to dealing with the customs man and my disposition was not improved by the fact that I knew I was carrying twice the quota of cigarettes, and I wasn't made any happier by his decision to charge me duty on *both* cartons of cigarettes. (Even at penalty rates though the cigarettes are cheaper than you can steal them in enlightened England. Not that I am against such high taxes on the weeds; as I frequently point out to some of my up-tight acquaintances who think that there is something immoral about a smoker, I'm willingly paying for the National Health to treat their stress-related diseases!) I suspect that the customs man was not a smoker and that he felt he was striking one more blow for purity when he extracted my money from me. His left eyebrow conveyed a distinct impression of grim satisfaction.

I toyed with the idea of presenting myself as more eccentric than I really am. (Don't want your comments on that.) With a suitcase full of purple clothes and stacks of typewritten paper (which I guarded with fierce protection) I had a lot going for me and thought he might wave me on as a 'crazy'. Forced to wait in the inevitable English queue until the customs man was ready for me, I of course took out my soothing purple knitting (which increased considerably in the air) and was stoically doing my one row purl, one row plain, when my turn came – and he asked me what I was knitting. When I told him nothing – that I could only do two stitches and couldn't follow patterns but that knitting calmed my nerves and stopped me from smoking so I just knitted until the wool ran out – the left eyebrow went into action once again. And he examined my knitting very closely; then held up very carefully every sheet of paper to the light. The whole process took two hours.

I think he was looking for something.

I've always worked on the premise of avoiding extremes if you want to avoid the attention of the customs man. Have noticed that it is usually those who appear the most 'radical' and those who appear the most 'conservative' who attract notice. I think I'll now have to include 'those who wear purple' on the list of suspects. I did have to acknowledge that with my purple hat, coat and boots, dressed in purple jeans and jumper, and carrying purple bag and purple rag doll, I didn't exactly melt into the crowd. What you don't need after that plane trip though is another three hours in the customs hall – and all that prying and questioning; (not to mention repacking the bloody suitcase; I explained to the customs man that you had sat on it to close it and that it wouldn't close unless *he* sat on it, but he was most uncooperative).

After him it was the English weather so it's no wonder I arrived home without a beaming smile. It might be spring here but it's a damned sight colder than the Australian autumn I left behind. The English do have a lot to contend with in the weather – no wonder they think that life wasn't meant to be easy and that hardship means a return to normal.

Not that it is a return to normal here at all. I didn't realise I was returning to a country at war. I am astonished. I must have adopted the Australian view of this 'international incident' because I had thought of it all as a bit of a joke – as the Australian newspapers portrayed it. But it's no joke here and I have had my share of culture shock since I returned. There are constant 'Falkland Specials' on the media – and they aren't supermarket bargains!

If anyone had asked me when I stepped off the plane what I thought the major war issue was, I would have said the safety of 'The Invincible', the aircraft carrier the Australians are going to buy from the British, because the Australians aren't prepared to take the name at face value – they think the ship might be scratched and they won't be able to afford the repairs. But 'The Invincible' and its individual fate isn't the issue at all here – it's all about the glory of Empire on this side of the world!

Being a colonial, I suppose it's not surprising that I don't share the British response to calls for the Empire. There is a real clash of images going on for me. Part of it is our female Prime Minister. She has been in the living room on many occasions since I got back and with what I could only describe as a 'deadly earnest-ness' has informed us all that 'British stock are under the heels of the invader' in the Falklands. It all happened too quickly for me. I have only been away six weeks and before I left, Argentina was a good trading partner (particularly when it came to the British selling arms to the Argentinians) and the Falkland Islanders had been ruled – by Act of Parliament – not to be British stock and not therefore eligible for British citizenship. But 'a week is a long time in politics' and I suppose six weeks is ample time for the world to be turned topsy-turvy.

But I find something very unnerving about that quiet, well-modulated, feminine – even maternal – voice of Mrs Thatcher, talking as 'commander in chief' about 'our poor boys – out there in the cold' and then stating the 'military options'. Too many contradictions. When Mary Wollstonecraft said that there should be more women in power . . . I don't think this was exactly what she had in mind!

Mrs Thatcher is ruining our old argument that if women were in power, things would be different. It's a bit inconsiderate of her don't you think? Some of us might even have to go back and do revised editions of our books now that we have a woman who does the job 'better than a man'.

I suppose I should be relieved that I haven't devoted my energy over the last few years to the task of getting more women into public office – on the grounds that wars would be less likely and the country would be ruled more compassionately. I would be having a crisis in confidence now as I watched the country *with two women in charge* (don't forget the Queen), go to war and deal so cynically with unemployment. It would mean more than revising my arguments – I'd have to revise my life!

I think we just have to accept that power does funny things to people. Look what it's done to men! Oh well, the end of another ideal; what's the next priority on the agenda?

My light relief (which could well be called my capacity to hide my head in the sand) has been Eleanor Dark.* I think she is the best woman writer I have read for ages. (I get pretty mad when I realise her books were there while I was studying Australian Literature – and I didn't even know she existed.) There's only one thing that's worrying me though as I try and analyse what makes her writing so good – do you lose the ability to appreciate the whole when you start breaking it down into parts? It was such a marvellous experience reading her trilogy on Australia that I would hate to do anything which interfered with the process. And I am so wary after having become proficient at proof reading; it has completely ruined my ability to read poetry any more. If I start examining Eleanor Dark's punctuation and vocabulary, do you think I'll stop seeing the wood for the trees?

After reading her you couldn't go along with the idea that

---

* Eleanor Dark. Australian woman writing about women in the 1930's and 1940's.

19

Australia is devoid of 'culture' – or even that it is a brash or brutal culture. (I am forever facing English people who allude to this deficiency – usually with the aid of a left eyebrow of course.) But when you read her there isn't even any excuse for the Australian 'cultural cringe', and Australians probably wouldn't suffer from the complaint if they were more familiar with some of their brilliant and sensitive *women* writers. Come to think of it, most of the evaluations of Australian culture are based on the contributions of males (surprise, surprise) and I don't think I would want to enter a debate arguing for their excellence. Actually 'cultural cringe' is probably justified if you use the contribution of the boys.

All that mateship! Man versus the elements in the outback – all the drinking, gambling, fighting, brutality, that are so often held up as *the* Australian cultural mores. It's hardly what half the population were doing at the time. . . But it is what is so often seen as characteristically Australian. Could it be that women have not had a voice, I ask myself? Perhaps this is evidence of a male-dominated society!

I have just been thinking about Australian (and New Zealand) women writers . . . I have made a list. It's pretty impressive. Miles Franklin, Christina Stead, Kylie Tennant, Eleanor Dark, Katherine Mansfield. Can you call Henry Handel Richardson an Australian? She didn't go willingly and I think she returned to the left eyebrow culture as soon as it was possible.

You know, given the size of Australia (population) – it isn't that it is *without* its art forms; when it comes to the female of the species women have been spectacularly successful in creating a superb cultural identity and art. Wish I knew more about some of the aboriginal culture and art though. If ever you see a book on it . . . send post haste, although I suppose that is a remote possibility. (The book, I mean.)

After Eleanor Dark I had to return to the post. What will I do with it all? It extends along the hallway so I am even having difficulty ignoring it. Lizzy and Renate have to some extent earned my undying love by opening and sorting it – but I would have subscribed to the 'ignorance is bliss' philosophy if they had chucked some of it! Lizzy has stacked a pile, three feet high, and stuck a label on it – 'Requests'. Thought there might be an invitation to have tea with the Queen so took a peek; wish I hadn't. Requests to act as referee, to provide research details, to recommend reading lists, to help with publication. And there are 46 requests for comments on manuscripts. *I* request a solution. What will I do? I have already ruled out the possibility of jumping off the Albert Bridge . . . the water is too cold at this time of the year.

It would take me at least one month and twelve hours a day to go through them. Can't and won't. Need to know more about technology . . . is there a word processor which *reads* the letters and then replies?

I'm itching to start writing 'There's Always Been a Women's Movement' but feel I have first to do something about all this post. Should I start writing? Should I do some of the post? I can't toss a coin – I keep cheating and end up with the answer that I should start writing. But I feel such enormous guilt. I know I could say that in part it is my own fault – that I don't come out and say just how huge the post has become and that I can no longer answer it. I would feel so awful saying that to women. (I want to be liked!) Of course, if *you* were willing to come over and explain for me, to say what a nice person I was, but how the task had become impossible – I'd willingly raise the money for your fare.

The other solution that occurs to me is an arrangement with the postman. He complained this morning that he delivers so many letters here it makes him eligible for early retirement. Perhaps I could persuade him to retire – or not deliver the post.

I miss you. I still haven't adjusted to your absence and have gone to speak to you on more than one occasion. I feel silly when I realise that you are more than 12,000 miles away and unlikely to answer. I have been on my own since I got back – Ted took off somewhere hours after I arrived. I don't think the two are connected though. He didn't look all that well but I resisted the temptation of asking whether it was because he missed my home cooking! He probably doesn't feel well because now I'm back *his* workload will increase. Oh dear, am I a burden to my friends?

And how is it for you? How have my nephews adjusted to my

departure? I must say it will be of benefit to my pocket not having to pay them piss-off money all the time so that they will go away and leave us to work. Did such crude, capitalist childbearing practices do any damage to their psyches?

I have another question; *are your scales accurate?* I know I put on some weight in Australia (and that it was the drink, not the food that was responsible) but according to my scales I am 8lbs heavier than when I left. That seems a lot. It means an *effort* to get rid of it. I suppose I could decide once and for all that I won't use the scales to measure my self esteem – but that philosophy doesn't seem to work for me. My self esteem is related to society's idea of the desirable weight!

Must face the real world and put aside this epistle to you. It does seem unreal that you are so far away and that it will be a week before I hear from you, and we get back into the sanity of sisterhood by post. But I'd dearly love to sit here and just keep writing . . . not even necessarily to you. Since we both listened to those tapes I made with Dora Russell I really do find myself wanting to drop everything else and to start writing and shaping them for the book. I'm beginning to feel almost desperate about it. But there are other tasks first . . . Why can't I just sit here and write and call for room service to make the coffee and answer the post? Hardly politically correct I suppose.

Coogee, April 1982

Dear Dale,

Back to the 'old' typewriter. Your rented typewriter has been taken away just as I had become used to the self-correction and was beginning to believe that my typing was improving. A vain hope, I am afraid. The only change in my typing has been that I now make the same mistakes at a faster rate than I did a year ago. I can, however, convince myself that the weather was in the hands of the goddess while you were here. The promised 'cold snap' (do you think men made up the term?) has developed, and I am pleased that the positive memory of Australian weather (at least) will go with you to England. It is nice to preserve some of the myths.

I was wondering, after you had left, (and I may have been drunk and maudlin because I came home and finished the bottle of wine we had been drinking at home) just how the reality of 'home' gelled with the myths. Do you still think of Australia as home or has London replaced it?

I remember feeling ill-at-ease when I first came back here in 1981 after the few years in Canada. Did the newspapers always have sport as front-page news? Did the casual dressing habits that I remembered as being so free and easy, always consist of a navy-blue singlet over a beer gut? Were Australian men always so crass and so intent on having a drink 'with their mates', and were Australian voices always so loud? I think now that the images of Australian men must have been there before I went away but I had forgotten them in favour of the myths. Really I have looked quite conscientiously for examples of the tall bronzed variety of Australian male but have yet to set eyes on even one of them. By the way, did you know the reason for Australian men always 'coming' so quickly? . . . They are all in such a hurry to get to the pub to tell their mates about it! Good Australian joke. Says a lot doesn't it?

In spite of my concern over myth and reality, we have settled back into routine here since you left. For me that means more sleep, less stimulation (you can see that I've already resorted to the weather), less wine; and for the children it means less money, closer supervision, fewer chocolates and a general decline in family goodwill. Jay has embarked upon a series of traumas over his homework and without the diversions provided by his 'maiden aunt', he seems to have become obessed about either doing or not doing his homework.

You know he is given a homework sheet every Monday with a certain amount of work to be done – supposedly each day – and the end product is to be presented for inspection the following Monday. You know too that I have made it a policy to stay right out of his personal organization of time. Well, we seem to have come to an impasse. He makes no effort during the week to do the work, I refuse to mention it more than once a day and consequently, Monday morning has become like a bizarre scene from Bedlam. Tears and trauma at eight o'clock on Monday morning are not the best accompaniments to an ordered life and I am being sorely tempted to interfere and to establish that he must do some work every day – for his sake and for my sanity.

So far though, I haven't said (yelled) anything. My reluctance to order his life is based on the firm belief that if I solve his problems for him, he will never learn to solve them himself and in this case on the equally firm belief that the homework he is being given is totally useless and extremely boring. It amazes me that even though we know how easily kids are turned off by performing tasks that are irrelevant to their lives, we risk killing their intellectual curiosity at eight years of age by expecting them to write out their times-tables, three times each, each day of the week. What's the point? Self-discipline? It can't be anything to do with learning their tables because they have to know them in order to write them out in the first place. It really riles me. There are probably thirty other mothers in Coogee at the moment worrying about the same issue and like me, they'll probably try to solve it by dealing with their kids rather than with an education system that doesn't accommodate the needs and interests of kids. I think I'll resort to your 'psychology' and simply pay Jay in hard cash to do his homework, thereby avoiding the whole issue . . . am not sure if I can afford it.

I watched the news last night (put the children in the bath while it was on rather than pay them to 'piss off' as we did while you were here) and the '*WAR*' it seems, is in full swing and, according to the media, with full justification. What is the attitude over there? I find it hard to believe that it is just being accepted as inevitable.

We are not at war here but do have our own brand of thrills. The cold snap has brought with it some heavy rain which poured into Karen's (the Monday to Friday lodger) bedroom. Fortunately, it did not direct itself towards her artwork and instead poured down the walls onto her bed. We had to shift the bed to the centre of the room and she had to evacuate the room in order to finish her work. At the moment, it has stopped raining, the bed has dried and we can move it back into position. All I can do is hope that is does not rain again for the rest of the year . . . I always knew I would be a philosophical repair person!

Aaron is not suffering like Jay with the loss of pocket-money. He is, as usual, treading very warily, eating lots of macaroni (which he cooks for himself – and is in the process of learning to do post-cooking cleaning) and is, not surprisingly, getting rather fat. I hope the macaroni fad does not last too long, for while I am only too prepared to encourage the do-it-yourself approach to eating, I am not at all keen on encouraging an overweight child. It's probably as much my 'puritan streak' that you have identified as a fear for his health. Why should I take care with what I eat when he can indulge in such blatant calorie consumption? Perhaps I can 'do a mum' and unobtrusively turn his attention back to fresh fruit – the kitchen would stay a lot cleaner.

I spent the night after you left composing the two entirely different applications for acceptance as a student-at-law. I had no trouble writing the 'cheeky' one. I explained in it, quite simply, that as an Australian female I had been well-conditioned into accepting teaching as 'a good job for a girl' and that it wasn't until I had been a teacher for some time that I realized that I had been tricked out of competing with my male peers for the few prestigious and better paying careers. Implied that it was an obligation that all institutions had to compensate women for their past treatment and used the anti-discrimination legislation to support the argument. I mean, if 'the law' encodes justice for women, who are selection committees to disagree?

I had a bit more trouble with the 'straight' application. Not surprisingly, I suppose, I was far more self-conscious trying to anticipate what 'they' would *like* to hear and see. It's a little like women and writing. Wasn't it Adrienne Rich who said women writers have to be constantly aware of a male audience when they write, while men rarely if ever have to really consider women when they sit down to 'create'. Shades of Norman Mailer and the one thing a writer needs is 'balls'!

The end result of my efforts was my presenting both applications to the Dean of the Law Faculty with what I considered a charming smile and the comment that I thought the two applications would provide evidence of my ability to adapt to circumstances. He advised that I submit only the straight one but I hope my efforts will result in a positive recommendation from him. After all, having the skills required to vary the 'truth' should be qualification enough for being a lawyer.

I did realise though, while I was composing the applications, that each of the pictures I painted really did reflect a part of me . . . One is the serious, more thoughtful (you would say puritanical) part of me, and the other is the irreverent, cynical person who won't accept that the world has to be the way it is. I wonder if being aware of different facets of oneself is a female phenomenon? It's the opposite of male 'tunnel vision' and of the rigidity of thinking and perception that I associate with men. Perhaps women have to have several dimensions of 'self' in order to present different faces to different men as we negotiate our way through male territory? Or is my serious side starting to show? Perhaps the explanation lies simply in me providing myself with some comic relief from the responsible mother image!

I have enclosed a copy of the review of '*Man Made Language*' that I found whilst reading through March 1982 edition of '*Refractory Girl*'. I suppose I shouldn't be surprised to find your name just about everywhere I look, but I still get a jolt and what can only be described as a 'flush' (a hot flush?) when I see one of your books in the bookshops, or encounter an article or a review in a magazine or journal. I might also add that I get extremely defensive if they reveal a lack of proper respect as this one seems to do. It sounds to me not only suspiciously academic but relatively obscure. Perhaps the two qualities are more closely associated than I like to admit.

I must add just before I go that one part of the homework that Jay did get done this week was a 'short essay on Anzac Day'. He explained that it was a day when wreaths (spelled reeths) were laid on the Cenotaph (spelled senotarf) to remember all the women who had been raped in war. Only a little of my input. I suppose that the rape issue is the only context in which he has heard the wreaths discussed and perhaps he remembered the march in Canada where we each laid a single flower on the cenotaph. Wherever it came from – I did not add that there were other reasons for wreaths on cenotaphs. I don't think a few alternative 'truths' will do him any harm. I shall let you know what comments (if any) are provided by his teacher.

Chelsea, May 1982

I feel that every letter should begin with a war bulletin. You might be free of the news from the front down under, but over here it is impossible to avoid. The whole nation appears to be revitalised by it . . . which says something about human beings, doesn't it?

Is it because I am a 'spectator' that I feel so detached? (After being harassed in the pub by that specimen of Australian manhood I have ample evidence that I am not a pacifist – so that cannot be the reason for my failure to become involved in the glories of war.) I'm very conscious at the moment that this is not my country of origin and that calls for Empire strike a different chord in me; perhaps jingoism is more readily inflamed among the native born and were it an Australian 'call to arms' I might well be out on the hustings. I doubt it though. I find the whole scene sickening and see no reason to alter my long held view that war is a boys' game. (One of the worst features is the enthusiasm in the eyes of many of the men at the prospect of finally testing out their toys to see if they work. I bet pounds to peanuts that after this little incident – and assuming that Britain does not become an Argentinian colony – we will have a whole spate of reports on which toys worked well and which ones need to be returned to the drawing board.)

I have been writing to Dora (Russell) fairly regularly because I know how distressed she is by the whole business. It must be dreadfully difficult to spend your entire adult life working for peace (seventy years in her case) and then to see all that work come to nothing. Again. But I think the pattern is unlikely to change; women have little chance of promoting peace while men control war!

For Dora this damned war is another bloody good reason for all sensible people to become feminists; she sees it as yet another example of the triumph of men's values (dominance) over women's values (co-operation). I think she was beginning to believe that some progress was being made (that is where *we* part company I might add). Now she has to face the fact that nothing has changed – no wonder she feels so depressed and desperate about it all.

I can be facetious about it at times but I still find it hard to come to terms with some of those grim statistics. So many killed, so many young lives gone – wasted – and they can't be replaced. All announced in such a neutral manner. It's partly because those who make the decisions – and the announcements – are so far removed from the reality, and the consequences.

If Margaret Thatcher and the Conservative Party are so keen on fighting as a solution, then I feel that they should lead it; there is much to be said for Henry V being at the front of his troops when he went into battle . . . At least he faced the same risks as his men and was not likely to disregard the consequences. The prospect of death concentrates the mind wonderfully I believe; a good old English proverb but one which is obviously selective.

There is a real split today between those who push the button and those who do the dying. The only version of the war we hear about is from those who survive it. It's like unemployment. Have you noticed that all the news, statistics, strategies about unemployment are provided by those who are employed? As soon as you are unemployed you cease to exist – you have no voice, become invisible; no longer a worker, a trade unionist, a 'man in the street'. Not what I'd call a free country when those who occupy the safest place are the spokespersons for violence and war, those who are employed speak for the unemployed – and of course those who are male speak for women! How about we all start speaking from our own circumstances? That *would* be a free press. It would also make existing media controversies about political bias look like a polite palace tea party.

I don't know. It all seems so simple to me sometimes. Those who have the power taking the right to speak for those who are out of power. My definition of oppression. Seems that I don't state my case very well though. Thanks for the review of *'Man Made Language'* but I have to admit that I don't understand it. From what I did read (and understand) it looks suspiciously like a review of a book I didn't write – and that the one that I did write can be dismissed in a few words. Not that I am upset by it . . . just find it tedious to have to look up so many words. Do you know any vocabulary-improving exercises for me?

Reviews. They are funny things, aren't they? I wonder how they ever developed into their present form. I'm not sure whether I made an independent decision to disregard them, or whether I have been forced to adopt that attitude as a means of self protection. My way of dealing with them is to treat them as research – a technique that has helped me in a variety of circumstances. (Do you remember that time when an eminent man was calling me neurotic, embittered, frustrated and frigid, and I started to make notes and asked him to repeat his statement so I could be sure of getting it down correctly – and then thanked him for being such a cooperative subject for my research on the ungovernable frenzy of males? Did he die from his apoplexy or survive for the benefit of future feminist researchers I wonder?)

I think there has to be some way of protecting oneself from the licensed malice which is the rationale behind many a review. (Reading Virginia Woolf's diary and appreciating just how hurtful and harmful she found many reviews, makes me think there is no immunity.) Any little peevish person (who has the right contacts) can deliver a diatribe against a writer on no good grounds other than the use of exclamation marks, appearance, or the place of residence.

Did I tell you about the recent review of *'Invisible Women'*? Written by a 'friend' (who'd better remain nameless in this context). One of the things wrong with the book, she said, was it resorted to biological determinism as an explanation. I was astonished when I read it – particularly since one other reviewer had said that I ignore the possibility of biological differences. So I rang up and asked her what she was referring to. And do you know what she said? Of course, she hadn't found any such reference in the book . . . of course, she knew I wasn't into biological determinism. How could I be so silly as to think that? What had happened was that she'd reached the end of the review and had said only positive things about the book. Well, – 'everyone knows you must say at least one critical thing in a review' – and I quote directly – so she'd put in the bit about biological determinism.

Words failed me! I suppose I could explain it in terms of women's lack of confidence, but sometimes I wonder whether it might not be better if I just got plain mad with one of my sisters; *I* might feel better anyway. (I did decline to meet her for lunch next week.) But it seems to me that you just can't afford to take reviews seriously. Especially not those written by 'friends'.

Why don't authors have right of reply? Why don't I get the space to review her review? (Could go on forever I suppose – like one of dad's jokes; she'd then want to respond to my review of her review.) A reviewer can write the most arrant nonsense – without even having read the book – and there's nothing you can do about it. And even if literary editors did devote 'equal time' to author's replies, I know what would happen to feminists. We would be seen to be complaining – yet again. (You've got it – embittered, neurotic, and basically unable to get a man!)

It wouldn't be a case of FEMINIST EXPOSES WOMAN-HATING MAN OF LETTERS. Much more likely – NEUROTIC WOMAN REVEALS HER MAN-HATING PREJUDICE. So, I know what you are saying: it's a man's world . . . and what would I do with my life if men started to be reasonable? I might have to find another deserving cause.

But I have been doing some of the research you so wisely suggested. I've only been measuring the column inches of the reviews in the paper for the few weeks since I got back – but already there's lots of ammunition. (The goddess must be with us – or else men are so used to going unchallenged that they don't even bother to try and disguise their blatant sexism.) I rang the literary editors of a few 'respected' papers and asked them how much space they were giving to women writers in their review sections. Perfectly predictable response. They all said the allocation was fair. One said it was equal, and one prominent editor went so far as to say women are dominating the reviews! And the old story – 'Poor men are getting a rough deal these days'. Well, you know how I respond to that particular stereotyped answer . . . *gleefully.*

What happened when I asked who was doing the talking in mixed sex conversations? Well, it was the women of course. And then when you get to measure it you find that women get to talk about 10-20% of the time in conversations with men. A woman who talks about a third of the time is seen to be dominating the talk.

And what happened when I asked teachers who got their attention in class? Well, it was all equal, wasn't it? No preferences there. And you measure it and find that girls get about 10-20% of the teacher's attention. Any more, and the boys think it unfair – and go into revolt.

So what do you think I found with the reviews?

I would have predicted about 10-20% of the space went to women's books. Well, *it is less than 6%* of the column inches. And the reasonable editor who thinks that women are getting more than their share is one of the worst offenders. Poor boys! It really tells you something when they think only 94% of the review section is not enough, doesn't it? When 6% for women is too much you get some idea how much men think they are entitled to – as a fair deal. Not that I'll be able to tell them. I bet this is one piece of research on publishing that we won't be able to find a publisher for.

I knew it wouldn't be much space that women got – but even I didn't think it would be so little. (I suppose it fits in with some of the research on women writers who are selected for study in establishment literary courses – never more than 7% of the authors. And there are quite a few male academics who think 7% is too much.)

Found some other things we well. Generally when women's books are reviewed, they are lumped together; e.g. four women writers reviewed *en masse* in a small article on women's fiction.

Another case of 'and the rest are girls'.

It's a tedious task measuring column inches, but it has still been quite stimulating work. Wish you were here to talk about it. (Could be an improvement on being 'there' where we couldn't talk without two small boys interrupting us and wanting more food all the time.) Would very much like your opinion on enclosed article from '*The Observer*' which is aimed at proving that feminism, and women's writing, is but a passing fad, which has had its day.

What about the opening lines? 'The great days of feminist radical literature seem to be over. Betty Friedan, Simone de Beauvoir, Germaine Greer *et al.* combined in their best work a high level of scholarship with the excitement of new, or at least recently discovered ideas. Now the climate for innovation seems bleaker . . .' And so it goes on. Dreadfully dreary we women must be. Nothing new, nothing creative.

And not a single shred of evidence for such a statement.

In the same paper there is a review of Erica Jong's book on '*Witches*' and it ends with 'You begin to suspect that Miss Jong has taken to culling hemlock at the waning of the moon, or whatever, or because she has a nervous feeling that the fun in feminism, (perhaps even the money) is coming to an end'.

Makes me so cross. The two reviews of women's books and both of them trying to claim that it's all over. (Don't they know that men have been saying that for centuries? Every time a woman protests against male injustice, men declare it is passé; that was *last* century's or *last* decade's issue! I call it wishful thinking on their part, myself.) There is much more evidence for the claim that women's books are selling better than ever, that there are more of them and they are more exciting, more stimulating . . . look at the sales, and the reprints!

Anyway, I'm thinking of asking some of the prestigious papers to carry the following ad:

Applications are invited for reviewers of women's books. The success-ful candidate must be of malign disposition, firmly convinced that the world hasn't been the same 'good old place' since women began this disruptive struggle for human rights, and should be a dedicated upholder of the principle that women should be seen and not heard.

Owing to the pressure of space, the reviewer must be able to see that all women's books are much the same, and be proficient in summarising ten books by women in ten lines. For this reason sympathetic consideration will be given to those with a distaste for reading women's books.

In the interest of balance, priority will be given to antifeminist candidates.

No doubt some of the current reviewers of women's books would qualify for appointment.

It's not difficult to see why so many sensible women have written under male pseudonyms. From start to finish you get a better deal, as even Charlotte Bronte (hardly the world's greatest sophisticate) well knew. I'm resigned to the fact that it would be too much to organise that research we wanted to do on unsolicited manuscripts – but it would have been a lot of fun. Sending off the same manuscript, sometimes with a woman's name and sometimes with a man's (and sometimes with an Anglicised name and sometimes with a distinctly foreign one), to a number of publishers – and then comparing the 'rejection slips'. (Might have been a problem if it had been accepted . . . suppose we could have gone on with it, under a pseudonym of course.)

That nice neat little trick produced some of the most mind boggling information when I tried it out on teachers, using student essays. Like the old study that Philip Goldberg did in the 1960s; the same article but when authored by John Smith it was considered impressive and when authored by Jane Smith it was judged mediocre.

There were no exceptions you know. Talk about a total double standard. And there were so many extra penalties for girls and bonuses for boys. When the well presented article had a girl's name on it, she got no extra credit; (on the contrary, a lot of teachers made disparaging remarks about it being 'just like a girl' to put so much effort into the headings and the illustrations at the expense of the content . . . which was really very slight). And when the same article had a boy's name on it? Well, not only was the quality of the presentation superior, and worth so many more marks, but you could see that the content was absolutely excellent!

But it didn't work the other way. Same old double standard which means that there's always a reason for seeing the boys' work as marvellous and the girls' as not up to scratch. The first time I got teachers to rate an untidy paper – ostensibly written by a girl – and they penalised it, I wasn't all that surprised. And I don't suppose I was shocked the first time I gave the same untidy paper to them – ostensibly written by a boy – and they interpreted the untidiness positively – as evidence of 'divergent thinking', 'his pen just can't keep up with his brain'!

I was shocked though when I repeated that exercise again and again and got the same result every time. No teacher, female or male, feminist or antifeminist, ever departed from that line. Which just goes to show how deeply entrenched that double standard is – boys are bright and girls are goofy. (You know, don't you, that if some smart little researcher came round and tried the same trick on us, we'd both fall into the trap as well – even though we'd like to think we wouldn't. Unfortunately, knowing the value system doesn't help you to stop using it.)

When every one believes that what men do is more important, you can see what we are up against with women's books. It's the old dilemma that if you publish, or review (or study) too many women's books – you'll lower the standards!

That's why publishers are always worried about women's books and are surprised when they sell . . . even if they always sell, and keep selling. Deep down they believe that women's books aren't the real thing and that they are risky. There must be at least five publishers in London who last year made a profit out of women's books but I'm sure if you asked them they would all tell you – quite sincerely – that women's books don't sell. And it's no good pointing to the statistics. They'll just say that's *not* the normal pattern. Something funny is going on, and it won't last. Just wait and see in a few years time, then it will all be back to normal again – and women's books won't sell.

I've given up on the idea that people change their minds on the basis of education, or information. They change their minds when they want to, and not before. Look at me, married all those years, every day giving my husband 'lessons' about work hours and justice, about women's right to humanity and a fair deal – and he didn't change. Yet he had an excellent private tutor in me. He didn't change because he didn't want to, he liked things the way they were. And unless publishers want to change (and I haven't any evidence that they do) then no amount of information will make them see women's books as anything other than a minor and transitory genre for a specialised reading public – women. Look at romances! It's the biggest book market by far, and it's by and for women, and that's the reason that it has such low status. (Spy stories, detective stories, thrillers etc. aren't such low status.) There's evidence that more women write and more women read (and buy books) but it is still men who are considered the real writers, it is men who are the proper reading public; and a good publisher therefore, is one who concentrates on the male. Virago is just an aberration in these circumstances. It's something a bit funny, that no male publisher can really understand. They didn't keep women's books in print because everyone knew there was no market for them . . . and then along comes Carmen Callil, makes a successful business out of something for which there is no market – and I hope she laughs all the way to the bank. But the fact that it has been so successful has got a few publishers interested in hopping on the bandwagon while it's still around. But they all know that it is just like feminism – only a passing phase.

That's one of the reasons I have enjoyed my 'little old ladies' so much. When Rebecca West says she was a feminist in 1907 and hasn't heard a single argument since then that would make her want to change her mind, you can see just how much a passing phase this feminism it.

I was trying to tell Sue Lloyd the other day not to worry about all the harsh things that are being said about her – it's predictable. Has been going on for centuries. Did I tell you about her? I interviewed her for '*Spare Rib*' as she has just edited the last edition of the Thesaurus and has come in for some of the nastiest treatment imaginable. (I am full of admiration for her; she took three and a half years to do the editing!)

When she was telling me about it she was quite clear that it was purely on the grounds of being more precise that she decided to use 'human' and 'humankind' instead of 'man', because 'man' is such an ambiguous term. And she also decided to omit offensive words – before she even realised that the majority of offensive words are racist or sexist. So as a result of taking the task seriously and trying to be reasonable, she's ended up with a Thesaurus that uses 'human' as a generic term and which doesn't have any racist or sexist expressions in it.

And of course without their prominent 'man' symbol, or their racist and sexist expressions, a lot of reviewers are very put out, to say the least.

Sue certainly didn't expect such a savage response to her reasonable and scholarly approach. She thought she was being unemotional and apolitical. But it is very political (if not emotional) to remove 'man' from the place of primacy, and so the reviewers have responded in kind, with emotional and political tongue lashings.

We worked out that one reviewer could not even have seen the book – only the press release – but it didn't stop him from urging bookshops to post warnings that the new Thesaurus had been composed with unintelligible sexism. His major thrust (sarcasm!) was that the 'rich man' had been emasculated to become a 'rich person' by the stroke of the sexist pen. Really thoughtful, dispassionate and evaluative comments, eh?

I think Sue was taking it very personally, but I told her about all the women (or some of them anyway) who had been treated in exactly the same way – for centuries. and I launched out a bit on Matilda Joslyn Gage and it helped to restore Sue's spirits somewhat when I told her that Matilda had proved (last century) that far from being the rational sex, it was men who had displayed the most ungovernable frenzy in their conduct in the world. So we sat there for a while chalking up all the evidence we could think of on male ungovernable frenzy. A much better approach; it leaves you sane.

Sue said that she had been warned that there might be some backlash, so I defined it for her (in our terms) so she could use it in her next edition.

Backlash: the ungovernable frenzy, displayed by men to protect their interests and power, long *before* they are attacked, and not, as is commonly and conveniently suggested by many men, *after* some of it has been taken away.

Of course, patriarchy still wins, OK? The hysterical (or should I say penisolent) responses of the men have ensured that for the first time ever, Longmans has a reference book on its hands that is a best seller!

One columnist absolutely slated her and because she assumed he was serious in his objections, she rang him up to ask why he had said such dreadful things. And he apologised (on the telephone of course, not in writing), and said that she shouldn't be so silly, of course, he didn't really think that way, he was a reasonable and intelligent man and the Thesaurus was well done. But there's no news in giving praise. Didn't she understand he had a column to write and there had to be something controversial in it? So much for the art of reviewing, and the free and fair press.

I felt much better after talking to Sue but it didn't last. I had to come back to my desk – and I feel so guilty. So much post and so many requests – and I'll never get through it all I'm sure. I've pulled the telephone out so that I can at least uninterruptedly try to plough my way through it but I don't have any heart for it at all and would so dearly love to get on with some writing. Have decided that what I need is a secretary, but it isn't just the politics of having someone else do all the dirty work that stops me – there is a simple matter of payment. I couldn't afford one. Obviously the solution is to get a wife. I'm told they don't have to be paid.

I'm pleased the kids are missing me . . . even if it is for my money rather than my self. They would have to be the only two beings on earth for whom I could appear as a source of wealth. As a child I think it would have been superb to have had an aunt who came to redistribute the world's resources and who wasn't remotely interested in whether you had been good, or what you were going to spend the money on. (Are you sure their teeth are still there, though? I did sometimes suffer pangs of guilt over the possibility that they would all fall out after the consumption of so many sweets.)

The goddess knows what you can do about the homework problem. I think you just have to accept that schools are not places for learning but agencies for keeping kids off the streets (and they aren't even very good at that, these days. Have you seen some of the figures for truancy lately?) If you don't expect the kids to profit intellectually from schooling I assure you, you won't be disappointed. It is only if you get child minding and the cultivation of intellectual curiosity mixed up that you could become upset by such absurd homework.

I still haven't adjusted to the fact that you are 12,000 miles away – and I am prepared to say *that* is probably a true as distinct from a belief statement. At the moment I could well do with a jug of wine, and thou beside me on a desert island. No kids, no wars, no telephone, and where even unemployment means something entirely different. It doesn't sound politically correct though, does it? Suppose it is just another variation on living in a squat and drinking camomile tea.

Coogee, May 1982

Have had the most amazing feeling of goodwill this morning to lots of things, brought about, no doubt, by a combination of several incidents during the last twenty-four hours. I wonder if the goodwill would continue if I had to deal with the war at close range. It certainly has disturbed your view of the world.

I received your letter from London – the first since you left – and while the issues that you raised about the war left me with that now familiar feeling of futility in the face of the huge odds that women and thinking people are confronting (obviously for us the two terms are synonymous), it did not detract from the delight I felt at the resumption of 'dialogue' with a sister. Also, I am still in a state of mild euphoria as a result of brother Graeme and friend Penny having picked up the children at 5.00 p.m. yesterday and having spirited them away to the movies and to McDonalds. I had to expend a little energy in rationalizing the 'fast food' . . . a quick assessment of what else they had eaten during the day and whether or not they were in need of something more substantial. I resolved that a piece of fruit and a glass of milk when they returned home would suffice, and allowed myself to luxuriate in several hours of peace – not the least part of which is the freedom to plan what I want to do without being interrupted. It's weird that even when the children have been taken on a voluntary basis, I still worry about whether or not it's too much trouble for those who are looking after them. I suppose

I should convince myself, as Lorraine has done, that the current generation of children will be providing the pensions for this generation of adults, and that a little child care is the least that adults can do to contribute towards that. My reluctance to take on this rationale is probably related to the fact that after considering the ideas and information in your letter, I am not at all sure that we will still be alive, or that the kids will even have a chance to 'grow up'.

The goodwill has, however, remained with me. When the children arrived home, I was able to give them their milk and fruit (no doubt the apple cores will be under the bed in the morning). Graeme and Penny stayed and had something to eat here and we all listened to Drusilla Modjeska's programme on the ABC (radio) about Australian women writers. I taped it for you and will send it after I have recovered from the cost of sending the '*Intruders*' manuscript. Do you know I had a huge argument with the man in the Post Office when I wanted to register the parcel?

'What's its commercial value?' he asked.

'It doesn't have any' I replied.

'Well you can't register it' he said, *smugly*.

'Then how can I ensure that it will arrive?' I asked.

'You can't, unless it has a value' he said. . .

Some time later, I gave in, and wrote *one million dollars* on the registration form. I have since wondered what will happen if Customs insist that I pay duty on it!

I think you are onto something significant with your ideas about Australian cultural cringe. The women writers are superb but you know that Drusilla reports that Norman Lindsay was dismissive of the literature of the thirties, and it's unlikely that it was an accident that that was the precise time when so many women were writing! They were not given enough credit for their contribution, and still so few Australians know about the women writers that you mentioned. I would like to think that the programmes on the ABC might make a change, but I imagine that the call of the television far out-weighs the call of radio these days.

The other sources of my goodwill today are firstly – the

weather. (Should I feel badly about mentioning it when I know that you do not have access to the same sort of 'free' pleasures in London?) I was awake at five this morning – alert – obviously thinking about all the work that I have to do (it's a big task to change the world), came downstairs to the study, and with the dog and the cat I watched the sun come up and felt the gradual warmth of the sun seeping into the room. Even the morning hassle when the children woke up – you know the routine – who is having juice and who is having a cup of tea, who had what on toast yesterday, and who is having what today – along with the dog needing to be taken for a walk with pooper scooper, and the cat needing instant gratification from the morning tuna fish fix, didn't totally eclipse the quiet appreciation of something as simple as witnessing the sun come up.

The other positive happening came out of calling in at the new hairdressing salon near Jay's school. After I dropped the kids off, I called in and had my hair trimmed by a young woman who made me feel a real sense of pride in women. She is from Port Macquarie – the far north coast of New South Wales in case you have forgotten, and explained that she has come to Sydney because she is aware that there is nothing more for her in Port Macquarie than there had been for her mother, and her mother had 'solved' all the problems, leaving the daughter with little in the way of challenge. Helen, the hairdresser, has set herself up here, is taking on the world (she is also an excellent hair-cutter – my hair is sufficiently difficult to prove this at first cutting) and is delighting in what I can only call a *power* to get things done. That's a communicable 'add-ease' (as opposed to 'dis-ease', of course) and I felt really positive about the world by the time I got home.

I also had a phone call from a national paper, asking if I would do an 800-1000 word article on '*Intruders*' – especially in relation to the Australian situation. The editor to whom I spoke could not guarantee that the article would reach final publication but seemed to think it would be ideal for the book section. Of course, I jumped at the opportunity to actually reach a bit further than the converted, and now have another task to keep me at the typewriter. I suppose the idea that some of the 'private' work might move into the 'public' arena is an attractive one – even if a little frightening.

And now – for a confession. I went during the week, with Sue, to see '*Reds*'. I thoroughly enjoyed it – in part because of your 'old ladies', Dora and Rebecca, and the recognition in what they said, of some of their idiosyncracies (what Rebecca said about the Webbs, for example). The other reaction to '*Reds*' – and the one which has prompted the confession – was that I hurtled myself startlingly into what can only be called a 'heterosexual' fantasy . . . produced no doubt by the combination of Dianne Keaton, Warren Beatty and my own current paucity of emotional, intellectual (dare I say sexual?) encounters with a person (apart from yourself) whom I like, admire and find generally stimulating. Quite a physiological (and, of course, psychologically) induced awareness of a dimension totally lacking in my life at the moment. It has occurred to me that the new underwear that you provided to replace the tattered remnants of cheap Canadian haberdashery, may well be instrumental in my 'awareness', and that I will get over it – one way or another.

I have somehow accumulated about eight books that I want to read in the next week – including a more careful reading of Emma Goldman – another '*Reds*'-inspired activity. Did she 'withdraw' from the revolution after her return to Russia? Was it because she saw the revolution developing into just another one of men's games rather than serving *human* ends? I remember from the typescript of '*Women of Ideas*' that she was involved in some sort of violence – I must look it up.

By the way, I did not like 'Jack what's-his-name' being cast as Eugene O'Neill in '*Reds*' – not because I have any preconceived notions about what O'Neill should have been like, but because he just did not qualify as the sort of man – physically or intellectually – whom Louise would have found attractive. His bum was too big. Projection of my own fantasies, I suppose, but I think O'Neill should have been someone small, non-macho, artistic, and with a depth that 'Jack-whosy' had no chance of portraying. There, you see . . . I told you that the heterosexual 'thing' had affected me. Perhaps I should go to see a good 'woman's' film to put me back on the rails.

43

Meanwhile, I must turn my broad shoulders – and dare I say 'broadening' mind to the events at hand. I am always aware that the children will be home within a few hours and I will have to don my other – serious – cap. The only way I can establish a balance between my conditioned tendency to negate myself in their interests and my need to assert that self in my own interests, is to keep telling myself that in the Australian context, I am the most radical person I know – and it has to stay that way . . .

I got a letter from you this morning which was one page long and which had neither beginning nor ending. It was basically a letter about why you shouldn't be writing a letter; did you leave something out, or is life like that?

I know that the objects and events of the world must all be circling and ready to attack, and I really do think about you and how hectic it all is on many occasions. How are you managing the two kids, the book writing, the promotion work, *and* the full-time degree? Want to write a book on '*How to be Superwoman*'? You might have some new ideas on it.

There is some reassurance I can give you though; give up the guilt on the fast foods because the goddess has been good, and I have some fantastic feminist news for you.

I got an article in for the journal this week and it is one of those rare ones which makes all the shitwork associated with the journal more than worthwhile. It is from a woman who is into nutrition (I think they called it Home Economics in our day), and who wanted to find out how and why women are kept in the kitchen. Oh, it is glorious!

She started with recipes from earlier this century, when women were doing the cooking without the miracles of modern technology. She doesn't say what the food tasted like, but she *has* helped to establish that on average, women have spent about the same amount of time across the centuries, preparing the family meal. (You know I also love research which just assumes that upper class women are an exception!) Most people would no doubt be surprised by her findings as with our deeply entrenched idea of 'progress', there is the presumption that things always get better . . . But here, (once again for women) the verdict is – no change!

I suppose that the explanation has to be in part that as the technology has become more complex (note that I will not use the word 'improvement'), so too have the recipes, with the result that the 'finished product' has to be much more elaborate to be acceptable today, than it needed to be in times past. Even if that was all that she had established, it would have been a worthwhile finding, and would have sat comfortably with some of the American documentation on housework – that the hours spent on it over the last one hundred and fifty years haven't varied much, despite all the so-called labour saving devices. But she adds more, and I am sure it will be soothing balm to your guilt-wracked soul.

She still wanted to know why it is that women are induced to spend so much time in the kitchen, and she suspected that it probably had something to do with the image of the 'proper' wife and mother, who carries the burden of the healthy family on her shoulders . . . and on her conscience. So she did some very nutritional research and analysed the value of the family meal in a number of households over one week, and compared that with the value of fast foods – from hamburgers to fish and chips.

And you guessed it. There was far more nutritional value in the fast foods than in the family meal – which makes sense if you think of the food in terms of freshness and of the British penchant for boiling vegetables to a pulp. Once more, we are into absurdities . . . all those women chained to the kitchen, in the name of family responsibility, when it seems that the kids would be much better off with McDonald's hamburgers. The rationale behind this particular absurdity is fairly obvious I think . . . if those women weren't in the kitchen they might have the time and energy to work for the revolution. I never cease to be amazed at how many convenient myths can be constructed – like the necessity of the family meal – on the basis of little or no evidence. Oh, are we gullible!

In the name of the health of the next generation, I think you should insist henceforth on fast foods only for the kids.

I just shook with laughter as I read the paper. You know what my opinion is of English culinary expertise and the persistent notion that if it is hot, then it is a good meal. I still get greeted by exclamations of horror whenever I admit that it is years since I have eaten cooked vegetables, and that I almost never depart from my salad diet (and speaking of diet, it is still 8lbs – what shall I do?). The English seem to think I should fade away to a shadow . . . I should be so lucky!

Anyway, I now have more ammunition for my allegation that school dinners are a plot against the working classes. Obviously it *is* fish and chips that is required . . . and not boiled, cabbage and jam rolypolys or whatever they are. Couldn't possibly campaign here at the moment though for an end to school dinners in the name of justice . . . that would really brand me as crazy.

Crazy enough having a relationship with one's sister . . . can't go round adding to it. (Oh am I tired of trying to explain you and me . . . and they say lesbians have problems because their reality is not confirmed; incestuous lesbianism is too much.) I can well understand your response to '*Reds*' and know exactly what it is to be seduced by the romantic myth. What keeps my feet planted firmly on the ground is that I know while ever Prince Charming might try and reassure me that he wants nothing more than to look after me, I recognise that what he is really saying is that he wants nothing less than for me to look after him . . . completely! (By the way, how is the manuscript '*Not Made in Heaven*' going?)

We shouldn't really continue to be surprised that romance is presented so attractively . . . after all, it is only the packaging that it has going for it!

I really must learn to watch my facetiousness . . . it has been getting me into trouble again lately. I know quite a few people think I don't take feminism seriously enough as it is, and I have no desire to add fuel to the flames. But I got myself into hot water the other day; I simply could not stop laughing when the conversation turned to 'lapsed lesbians'. What do you think they are?

I extricated myself pretty quickly with a straight faced discussion on the side effects of female unemployment. . . when men own 99 per cent of the world's wealth, and women are increasingly facing unemployment, I should have thought it was perfectly predictable that there would be a return to the heterosexual fold. How else are women going to get their hands on the resources unless they do what they have always done? Even board and lodging in return for services rendered is better than no board and lodging . . . And if the alternative is homelessness (and the figures here for homeless women are horrendous), then I'd choose to be a 'lapsed lesbian'. Another area of failure for women is constructed.

I just can't see that lesbianism is any less of a social construct than heterosexuality . . . although I can see *why* lesbianism is for women the more attractive of the two. If relationships between the dominant and the oppressed are unsatisfactory, then there is much to be gained if one is oppressed from *not* having relationships with those who are dominant. But I can't go along with the idea that it is more correct, more real, or even more natural. In my terms it is just more sensible!

And I really do refuse to treat sexual preferences as a life or death issue. Not even men have been able to prove that they die from sexual frustration and they have been working on it for quite a long time. Of course, it *is* important in a society where basic needs are taken care of, and you don't have to spend all your time worrying about filling your tummy – or about avoiding the bullets. And of course I see that heterosexuality underpins many of the practices of male power . . . But I'll tell you what: I bet if all women were to be lesbians tomorrow, it would be no guarantee that male power would end.

I think at the moment I am more concerned about the implications of war and peace than about lapsed lesbians. I haven't heard from Gloria (my Argentinian friend), and I spend quite a lot of time wondering and worrying. I thought that even if the letters that I sent from England were being censored (or destroyed) the ones I sent from Australia would probably get through (*you* aren't at war with Argentina yet are you? Britain hasn't called on the colonies for troops has it?) I don't know what to do for the best; I want to make sure she is all right and hasn't joined the ranks of the 'disappeared' . . . although that is probably self indulgence. . . What could I do if I *did* find out? But I don't want to put her at risk so I guess I should leave it for a while. If she suspects her post to England could be tampered with, she might think it wiser to write to your address. If anything arrives could you let me know?

I am aware that the issues I get involved in sometimes don't make all that much sense in terms of the sum total of human affairs. During this last week I have had quite a few altercations with male interviewers and I have to stop and ask myself whether this is where my energy should go. (I got a letter from Dora yesterday saying she simply cannot understand how women can devote their lives to the pursuit of equal pay when the planet is at risk; I can quite appreciate her point of view but I also think that women must work on all fronts, and that there is no single issue – which won – would guarantee an end to male power. Suppose I should listen to my own advice at times.)

I went to Manchester for the centenary celebrations of Sylvia Pankhurst and, through a series of misunderstandings, committed the cardinal crime of allowing myself to be interviewed by a man. I should know better by now. From the time I set foot in the place, I could see the whole operation at work. The entire foyer was filled with blown up photos of the male heroes of the airwaves and there were purposeful men striding in all directions, while the only three women I saw consisted of one sitting at the reception desk, one pushing a polisher, and one doing a magnificent job of managing a male ego . . . (If she was being paid at the rate she was worth, she should have been earning a fortune . . . but I can hear your response . . . Don't be silly. *She was doing it for love!*)

I wonder how those very same confident men would feel if we took them into a building where the only visuals were of authoritative women, and where the few and only men were in menial and subservient roles. Do they know that they would completely lose their confidence before they even opened their mouths? The whole system of patriarchy has to be an arrangement that has *evolved* . . . Of all the men I know, *none* could have ever *set up* such a successful system. (It's enough to drive one to spirituality isn't it?)

Anyhow, seeing them all playing their little games, again, I was blowed if I was going to have my confidence eroded; politics demanded that every women should do her duty and I decided it was my duty to do my damnedest.

When the interviewer came out to meet me, it was all I could do to stop myself from giggling because I kept thinking of Elizabeth Cady Stanton's warnings about which men are the ones to watch . . . the short ones, going bald, with a prominent thrust to their chins and a tendency to 'preen'. The interviewer qualified on every count.

He began by kissing my hand, making a big show about his gallantry, and making a lot of noise about how much he *liked* women. (Do these men think we are fools? Of course they *like* women! No-one else looks after them so well, or makes them feel so good!) After these deliberately overwhelming and supposedly disarming preliminaries, I was left – on my own – in a room adjoining his studio, and where the only sounds to be heard were the soothing notes of his own voice on the air relayed by a very loud speaker.

Such isolation while the expert holds forth is almost guaranteed to bring about a severe case of nervous collapse, but I am pleased to inform you that nervousness was the least of my problems. It was rage pure and simple that started to make its presence felt.

Even as I listened, the man attempted to enhance his own image by talking about the celebrations for *Emmeline* Pankhurst. Apart from all his other foibles, he must have been illiterate, because he had the press release with Sylvia's name clearly written, directly in front of him.

Just before he was to begin asking me questions, I was hurried into the studio – and it is also unnerving to have questions hurled at you before you have time to get your breath . . . or even sit down! And from the outset, it was obvious that he didn't give a fig for Sylvia (or for Emmeline either for that matter), but that it was crucially important for him to be seen as enjoying some sort of sport, and victory, with me.

I went through all the usual pros and cons . . . quickly! Do I let fly and run the risk of alienating women, who will feel sorry for the man and who will want to rescue his bruised ego if I am lucky enough to deflate him? Do I want another diatribe against the embittered and cruel feminist? Or is it about time that women made it clear that we just won't put up with that sort of shit? Needless to say, I recited my feminist catechism . . . which insists that women have never got anything by being polite.

As he informed me, within the first few seconds, that his wife liked staying home to look after his children, and that these feminists were nothing but nasty, soured people – interested in making the rest of the world as miserable as themselves – I couldn't be expected to sit there and be deferential. Besides, what would Sylvia Pankhurst think? If she could go to jail over men's refusal to grant women their rights, I could not be coy in the face of such puny provocation.

It's the first time I have really cast caution to the wind when it has been a 'live' interview. I said I had better things to do than listen to *his* emotional hangups, and that *if* feminists were portrayed as 'undesirables' it was because there were silly little people like him in the media, etc. etc. He nearly fell off his chair and his (male) producer was a classic study in indecision as he weighed the pros and cons of pressing the button and switching to martial music. I can only conclude that the producer must have been having a feud with his prize disc-jockey because there was little evidence of the famous male bonding, and he just let the spluttering man continue, presumably on the grounds that given enough rope, he would hang himself.

I can report the good tidings that outwardly – at least – I remained calm, (the adrenalin was flowing and the heart thumping, but that was not obvious on the air waves), while our splendid male interviewer gave way to apoplexy, interspersed with bitchiness of the highest order. If I did nothing else I ensured that I won't be asked back again for more baiting. The producer, however, seemed to suffer conscience pangs after a while and ushered me out before the programme was scheduled to finish, muttering 'Really good radio' in a most unconvincing manner.

I met some women that night who had heard the interview and said they couldn't believe their ears at the time; there was a great deal of laughter when they recounted their astonishment, and much relief when they saw that I had lived to tell the tale. But such activities do take years off your life . . . I'm not budging again from my stance on *no* male interviewers.

(That's not quite true; If I could do some research on it I would be back in there . . . partly because with all these ethics floating around about research on human guinea pigs, you couldn't ask anyone else to subject themselves to such harassment, could you?)

I'm looking forward to listening to Drusilla's radio programme when you send it. I hope your finances have recovered sufficiently for you to be able to post it soon. I don't know if your manuscript has arrived yet – I certainly haven't had any complaints from Routledge that they have had to pay duty on a million dollar manuscript – Or horror of horrors! Did you send it to me?

I just can't make any more 'explanations' to the postman. He told me the other day (out of the kindness of his heart) that the security forces would be on to me soon if the person sending me these coded letters didn't desist. I presume he was referring to some of your cryptic comments on the envelopes . . . about England being a country at war, and what you think I should do about it!

Robyn [Rowland] has also been writing – but without the innuendo of espionage – and I am really excited about her book [*Women Who Do and Women Who Don't – Join the Women's Movement*]. I can hardly wait to see the completed manuscript. Her positive feelings about it might be some compensation for the negative things happening to her at work. What do you think about the latest refusal she got for her women's studies course? In a way, I think it is hilarious that they object to women's studies on the grounds that the university doesn't have enough counselling facilities for all the women whose marriages would break up. (They really said that, and it is in the minutes.) 'Ah, if only it were that simple,' says Robyn wishfully . . . 'we could have the revolution tomorrow!' I guess she has asked them about the facilities available for all the women whose marriages do *not* break up.

It is like the middle ages isn't it? You aren't allowed to raise certain topics or discuss certain questions because it will threaten existing social arrangements . . . and you can't have that! Sometimes I get so cross about these slogans of 'academic freedom'. And I get cross about the idea that behind every feminist is the evil desire to destroy society – it would be so easy to argue that we are motivated by philanthropy and social concern, and are completely 'innocent'.

I have never really sorted out to my own satisfaction why change is so disturbing. Perhaps because in some areas of my life I have never had to confront it . . . are you thinking of changing our relationship and moving on to another? I suppose that is one benefit of biological sisterhood . . . you never have to justify the choice. But then, that looks suspiciously like biological determinism, doesn't it? Maybe we are just fundamentally *incorrect*.

About the one page letter . . . Yes, life has been a bit like that recently – all bits and pieces and unfinished ends. I think perhaps it is a hang-up associated with mother's knitting, and knowing how quickly your 'work' can unravel if you don't finish and tie the ends securely. I have three major essays to do, a book to write, several articles at various stages of completion, and those two charming children who seem to know just which moment is the 'right' one to interrupt me. Yesterday, I was exactly at the point of formulating my final (and of course earth-shattering) thoughts about deconstructing medieval history, when shrieks from the back of the house alerted me that something was amiss. As it transpired, the handlebars of a bike had, *by accident*, lodged themselves up Aaron's nose. My medieval women had to wait!

I was absolutely delighted with the information about fast foods and nutrition. I considered it my mothers' day present (although *our* mother made sure that the children had a present for me). I found a card for mother – from you – and even though I thought you may have sent one from London, I gave it to her because it seemed so appropriate. It depicted a mother duck waddling sedately along with two well-behaved baby ducks in tow, and a third baby duck screeching to a halt in front of the mother, saying 'Happy Mother's Day'. Inside the card, the inscription was . . . 'From your dramatic child'. I thought you and she would appreciate the significance of the 'dramatic' child.

I enjoyed your comments about 'lapsed lesbians'. Of course, there is a connection with economics. I think one of the reasons that economics retains any credibility in the face of so much evidence that it is uneconomical, is that its inefficiencies can be used to advantage. The more the financial system is 'messed up', the greater rewards there are for those people in the top decision-making positions. I recently heard a 'successful' businessman state that at least a recession 'flushes out' the 'dead-wood' (peculiarly Australian terms, I suppose – and always the scatological imagery!). He did not take kindly to my pointing out that a recession could be seen as a means by which managers and owners reorganized their business to increase *their* profits at the expense of the workers who were thus deprived of work – along with their identity. 'Socialist propaganda' he said, 'What do you know about the *real* world?' . . . And I had to acknowledge that my existence is a mere figment of imagination, and that indeed there is nothing 'real' about me, about women, or about the world that women inhabit in Australia.

One of the articles I am preparing – at irregular intervals – is a paper for the ANZAAS Conference this year. It's the Australian and New Zealand Association for the Advancement of Science and it's being held at Macquarie University. The theme is 'Australia's Industrial Future' and as it is the first time that a Women's Studies Section has been included, there has been a call via the feminist networks for papers and presentations. I want to present a case, based on Virginia Woolf's observations, that almost everything that has been written *authoritatively* about women, has been written by men. My plea (humorous of course – not intense or embittered) is for support of Women's Studies journals and for a forum where women's own views can be circulated and given validity. Tell me how something as important as that can be put into a 'light' and amusing tone? It's a little like asking blacks to make sure that they sing, dance and entertain us while they state their grievances! Providing I solve the 'tone' problem, I shall send you a copy of the paper and any others that I think appropriate for the journal or for *Forum*. I know one woman is doing a paper on how *protective* legislation (for women in the workplace) has been a euphemism for *restrictive* legislation, and how it has served to keep women out of certain areas of employment. We have here a regulation that prohibits women from lifting certain weights (thus ensuring their exclusion from some of the better-paid jobs), while there is absolutely no restriction on the lifting of particular weights within nursing. I suppose that now the wages within nursing are becoming respectable, similar provisions will be brought in to 'protect' women and make jobs available for men! The irony is, of course, that no-one – male or female – should have to lift excessive weights. Does it strike you as peculiar that there are so many mechanical lifting devices available within the transport and building industries and absolutely none available within hospitals? Methinks there could be a connection!

Jay is sadly missing that instant money supply that you provided him with and wishes we were richer. Do you think he might acquire the perspective for an up-and-coming capitalist with all the 'right' tendencies? Aaron, less affected by the money, is still trotting off happily each day to The House at Pooh Corner, totally unaware that there are any alternatives to full-time day care. Do you remember me saying when Jay was born that *my* children would be kept out of institutionalized educational systems for as long as possible? (I think I even visualized 'teaching' Jay at home!) Well, Aaron has now been going 'to school' since he was three months old and at this stage the only effects seem to be that he is well-adjusted, aware, co-operative and easy-going. Do you think that Bowlby with his theories about maternal deprivation was hired by *them* to ensure that mothers would not – even if they could afford it – send their children to places where they might learn about co-operation during their formative years? Imagine what could happen to the system if we started producing children who thought that negotiation rather than confrontation was the way to solve problems. Total chaos.

I am at a loss to make sense of the Falklands. All those issues you raise about war ring true but I can't believe it is just that people are stupid and don't learn. Perhaps I am cynical but I feel there must be other dimensions to the fiasco that aren't being raised. (There I go again assuming that there has to be a rational and sensible answer to all questions – when everything else I know indicates that there is *no* rational and sensible plan.) Someone here suggested a dastardly connection between the Falklands oil and the Russians, (shades of Australia and the 'Yellow Peril'), and I would like to know more about that possibility. I hate to think that the whole thing can be explained in terms of political expediency and that young people really are losing their lives in order to create a diversion from economic mismanagement. Keep me informed. It's rather hard here to sort out the incoming information.

I feel a lot more at ease with your insights into reviews. They really do serve as another way of controlling knowledge, don't they? That figure of 6 per cent of space being devoted to reviews of women's books is staggering. I shall certainly start 'consciousness raising' here in relation to reviews and while I have a gut feeling that it must be 'better' here, I remember that I too believed for many years that women were the talkative sex.

I went to a meeting of the *Editors* – a group of people involved in publishing – where the evening's discussion was based on reviews. According to the editor of '*The Saturday Herald*' book pages (a woman, I might add) there *is* a connection between *reviews* and book *sales* – although she was not sure that the books sold by this means were always read. There was quite a lot of talk about reviews as a particular literary genre – used to sell papers and magazines rather than to sell the books being reviewed. The idea of the reviewer being the selling point – rather than the author of the original work – makes the whole scene rather bizarre.

Thinking about 'bizarre' reminds me that I have numerous chores to complete before the children arrive home. Karen (the lodger) is bringing home her male friend this evening – presumably for me to meet him. The idea of adolescent love being paraded before my very eyes in my own home is not an attractive one. It has too many painful memories. I suppose I should do what you have advised in the past and be grateful that I can remember all the errors and mistakes along the way. It seems such a waste though to watch other young women making the same 'mistakes' but I have to acknowledge women's personal experiences do not hold up against the myths that society and the media promote. I am working on *Not Made in Heaven* with this in mind but have yet to capture that elusive 'tone' that I want to create. I'll just have to persevere . . .

Missing our 'talks' but getting more regular sleep since you left . . .

Chelsea, May 1982

What a wipeout since I last wrote; I fully intended to continue with Part II of that letter after I went out to supper, but by the time I got back I was really ill, and took to my bed – only to have to emerge at regular intervals to make use of the toilet, for a variety of purposes. (I realise of course that I run the risk of confirming most people's suspicions about the scatological nature of Australians with this disclosure, but such upheavals – I use the word advisedly – do impinge rather dramatically on my otherwise ordered life.) Sometimes I even wonder about the positive features of my diet when things like this happen. I could, of course, take refuge in a reversal of Ted's standby argument – and insist that it must be something that I *drank*! (Given that the Italians are supposed to have produced more 'wine' last year than the grape harvest would permit, perhaps this explanation is not too far out; we *were* drinking Italian wine.)

Same old story to report on other fronts though; the post isn't completed and I haven't got down to writing as yet. Forty-five letters sent today, but the pile doesn't look any smaller. I haven't even got round to writing to Dora and I know how keenly she feels about the war, and how much she appreciates contact. Might still manage it before I get to sleep (what is that?), but lots of outstanding things to do on the journal before I can allow myself the luxury of a 'personal letter'. If we hadn't thought about the possibility of editing and publishing our letters (and some of them are going to need drastic editing . . . think of the libel) I might even be tempted for the first time to think of my letters to you as an indulgence. As it is, I can classify them as work and feel no guilt – Oh for the days when there was a dividing line between work and leisure, when I lectured on nonsense during the day and did the feminism at night . . . as a hobby. These days I have to stop myself from thinking that work is answering the post, and leisure is writing books. Some leisure!

Ted is just as busy. We'd have trouble explaining our 'relationship' to anyone who only understood the conventional ones. Friday night is still meeting night, the only time we get together to swap notes. At least we won't get tired of each other's company. We may have lived together for eight years now, but with less than only 50 contacts a year we haven't equalled the proximity of the average first year of conventional marriage.

Last night (before the adverse effect of 'the drink') we were talking about living arrangements, and I became aware for the first time that apart from mum and dad, virtually no-one I know has any arrangement that could really be called standard. Of course it could be that all my women friends are strange – a distinct possibility and one which has occurred to my critics when I have indicated that much of my research has been conducted on my friends. But even in our own family Ted and I don't qualify – seeing that more than half my friends have never met him and we have only appeared as a 'couple' on two occasions in five years. Without 'benefit of clergy' brother Graeme and Penny are out, and with the father of your children living five hundred miles away, you aren't exactly upholding the standards of the nuclear family.

But it goes further than that. I don't want to embarrass them so I won't mention any names, but among my women friends there is one who is married but whose husband lives in another country. Another who is married, has her own 'bed-sit', and moves between the marital flat and her own independent space. One is divorced but her husband lives across the road so the children can move between with the minimum of inconvenience. One lives and works in the country but shares weekend city dwelling with the father of her child. Another isn't married but has a long term relationship conducted from two flats . . . *His and Hers*. And these are just the 'hets'. Things get more complicated when you consider relationships among women.

Yet for women who have relationships with men there are really only two categories . . . single and married. (Owned or not owned.) And I find it remarkable that of *all* my women friends involved with men, not one of them could legitimately be placed in either of these categories.

I understand some of the reasons behind these departures from the 'norm'. They are the same reasons that Crystal Eastman and Vera Brittain gave earlier this century; if women want to ensure that they aren't responsible for *his* shitwork as well as their own, then the only solution is separate dwellings.

Despite the prevailing image of the media, it does look as though women *are* creating some alternatives for themselves and trying to establish arrangements where they don't automatically service men. But it looks as though we have another case of 'language lag' . . . for just about every woman I know makes a mockery of the terms 'married' and 'single'. I'm single and yet the way I live could I suppose in some circles 'pass' as married (goddess forbid, that would really be the end of my credibility), while the lives led by many of my married friends look suspiciously single. Any suggestions for new words which could adequately describe this present state of chaotic contradictions?

The current flexibility in living arrangements opens up all sorts of subversive possibilities doesn't it? What constitutes nepotism now?

I've always maintained that if we really took our feminism seriously we would start infiltrating enemy ranks. For so long we have argued against our invisibility – and the dismissal of women as manipulators – you know the 'Behind every great man there is a woman . . .' myth. Well, maybe we should be using it rather than fighting it . . . guerilla warfare.

Damn this promotion in the public world, and the affirmative action programmes (which leave women in a worse position after, than before); I think we should just start sneaking in through the heterosexual door. We could insist that the sign of a true feminist was one who was prepared to make the grand sacrifice for the cause . . . and establish an intimate (and of course manipulative) relationship with an influential man.

It might not be as silly as it sounds on the surface, you know. I have had a few surprises lately. One Vice Chancellor was making the right noises and I was informed (in a very low voice, and 'off the record' of course) that for the past six months he has been living with an active feminist, and since she moved into his private world, quite a few women have moved into his public world. Looks to me like a better strategy than working to get more women into parliament (Oh, does Mrs Thatcher complicate the issue! . . . I shouldn't expect that our strategies would be terribly useful on that front). Could give a new twist to 'management' studies if we started spreading the rumour that behind every great man is a conniving feminist.

Probably wouldn't get many volunteers for action though. Might have to make it a compulsory course for women's studies.

However, you can see what advantage has accrued from keeping the world in heterosexual order, and keeping women labelled 'Mrs' and immobile. I really do think we would have more going for us if we introduced a slight element of suspicion and fear into our public personas. Then we wouldn't mind if the newspapers gave us a bad press . . . when there really was some substance to their accusations.

Speaking of bad press . . . delighted that you have been asked to do the article for the newspaper. Is it just a coincidence, for I have been asked this week to write something for a paper over here? I'm looking forward to it. Maybe that's something we can be when we grow up . . . journalists. It would have saved a lot of time if we had thought of that 20 years ago, wouldn't it?

Of course I have no idea when I shall fit it in. I have so many unfinished projects that I frequently feel that 'blind panic' which means things are out of control, and I don't get everything done. Spend a lot of time in bed at night . . . thinking! Seems better to call it that, than *insomnia*, and also makes me feel more comfortable when people ask me when I get my thinking done. Used to feel terribly embarrassed that I couldn't give a time and place and was even tempted to say that I didn't think at all!

I promised that '*There's Always Been a Women's Movement*' would be finished by August and here it is almost June and I haven't even started to write it. And it isn't just a simple matter of writing up the interview material – I'll have to go and do quite a bit more reading to follow up some of the things that my five 'old ladies' (will they mind the terminology?) talked about. And I'll need to allow sufficient time for them to look over what I have written and to make any changes that they might want.

I've written the proposal for '*Time and Tide Wait for No Man*' and I'm trying to decide – realistically for a change – how long it will take me to read through about ten years of the journal (from the start in 1920 to about 1930), make a selection, get it xeroxed, and write the introductions and the link pieces. I have to take into account my endurance span working at Colindale (the newspaper section of the British Museum) – it is limited. Can't smoke. Ruins my concentration. Find excuses for not going there for the day.

And there is all the bumf I have to find out about copyright. I should do it *before* I send the proposal off for a contract (partly because permission fees can make a difference in the cost of the book). When are newspapers out of copyright? Is it fifty years, like people? Who owns the articles without names – the newspaper? And if so, how do you get its permission to reprint when it has been defunct for so many years? What's the going rate on fees for reprinting articles from newspapers from sixty years ago? So many questions. I do wish you were a lawyer already, although no doubt you can see some advantages in delay – I would simply dump the whole copyright business on you. No-one seems to know much about it, but a lot of people have 'opinions'. At the moment, I am not even sure that I can use the title '*Time and Tide*' . . . Maybe someone owns it. The problems of capitalism where you have to locate the owners of everything . . . even ideas.

Have also been thinking that we should map out a proposal for '*Sisters*'. If we are going to write it up at Xmas time we should at least know beforehand how long it is supposed to be and which publisher it is for, and we won't know that until we have a contract . . . which means a proposal.

Late one night last week, I spent some 'insomniac/thinking' hours and drew up some ideas for future books. I want to do that one on '*Women and Writing*', and I am still keen on '*For the Record*'. I have almost completed '*Feminist Theorists*' (and again have decided it is easier to *write* books than to *edit* them) and you know that I always want to have a list of exciting projects ready to start on. My continual fear that I will run out of things to say (despite the contrary predictions of my adversaries) is never far away, so it is reassuring to have about six possible books in the pipeline.

But as sure as eggs are eggs, I know what is going to happen. If I deliver the four books next year as well as the remaining two this year, there is going to be the inevitable article (somewhere), on the *superficiality* of the writing.

Either someone will start saying that I write very poor stuff, that quality is being forsaken for quantity (not that I have suffered from a surfeit of reviews on quality), or else I'll be accused of either (a) having a team of research students ghost-writing for me, or (b) there will be the suggestion that has been levelled at female writers since Aphra Behn . . . that there is a man somewhere behind the prose. Ah well, all I would like is to be able to get in beforehand, to write the review *now* that is bound to appear next year . . . but of course I wouldn't be able to get it published! Could I have it stored in a vault somewhere and bring it out at the right time and say 'Beat you to it', when the mandatory malignancy materialises? (Should ask Renate, she's Swiss; she should know whether Swiss banks have vaults for reviews and do this sort of thing.)

Can just imagine the response I would get from some of the literary editors if I went in now with a review of my next year's work . . . which stated that the standard of my writing had deteriorated. (Already one 'friend' has referred to me recently and with sarcasm, as the 'writing machine'. Personally, I think that teaching school was much more difficult and demanding than writing three of four books a year . . . and besides political-ly, I am all in favour of a return to cottage industries.)

Unless I get some of the present shit sorted though, I won't be delivering *any* books next year. The proofs of '*Women of Ideas*' will be here next week and I still want to do that index . . . and that will take quite a few weeks. The goddess knows when I will get down to proper writing again.

I always get a bit depressed when I am *not* writing but I think it's worse at the moment, with both Pippa and Renate away. It is the first time I have missed the National Women's Studies Conference in the States and although I am not sorry for a minute that I didn't go (the post? the writing?), I do miss them. Have had a few letters saying that they are thoroughly enjoying themselves and Pippa should be home in the next week or so but Renate is staying on to do her book on *'Theories of Women's Studies'* with Gloria at Berkeley.

Do let me know how the ANZAAS Conference went, and whether there are any papers we should follow up for the journal; (Is anyone doing a report for *'Forum'*?) The BSA Conference (British Sociological Association) went well . . . even in my absence. Some of the papers seem excellent and I have sent you separately a copy of Liz Stanley's paper . . . I loved it, but I think quite a few people will probably by upset by it.

Liz persistently argues that as feminists we shouldn't just be asking *Why* men are into dominance but *how* they do it, and of course I couldn't agree more. I have no idea why men want to be king . . . and no need to know why it all started, although I do favour the theories about male jealousy, necessity for compensation, and absence of a justifiable role in society. If I'm going to be able to take preventive measure then what I need to know today is *how* the boys can convince the girls that boys are superior, when they have no evidence to support them. Like 'Sophia' (remember her? 1739?) I want more than the bare words of those who advance the case for male supremacy . . . in the interest of reason and logic.

Most of my research has been motivated by *how* in some way or another . . . *how* do boys manage to dominate in conversation, *how* do they get so much attention in school, *how* are they able to rewrite the historical record so that only their own actions are featured? These questions all seem sensible enough to me (and they are certainly productive at times), but then I don't have any set ideas about what is suitably 'theoretical' and I'm not particularly intimidated by someone who insists that they have a monopoly on 'theory' and I don't qualify.

Really the reason I wanted to do *'Women of Ideas'* and *'Feminist*

Theorists' for that matter, was because I think women have been told that theorising is something that men do and that women by definition are incapable of, so I'm not all that impressed when informed that there are rules about what is a theory and what is not. I know that quite a few people think that the only sort of theory there is, is that which is concerned with *why*, and that poor old *how* is just an impoverished and inferior relation . . . to do with pragmatics, or expediency. If that is what you think, then there is no way to explain Liz's stand . . . because it isn't theory. Simple isn't it? Someone sits and decides what theory is and who can and can't do it . . . and if you don't conform, you are non-data, invisible.

As with my research, there are probably a lot of places that Liz wouldn't be able to get her paper published . . . not sufficiently 'scholarly', or 'theoretical'. But these are just political terms for keeping women (and our questions) out of the records. That's partly why I delight in Liz's paper . . . she breaks all the rules and smiles as she does so. There's nothing worse than uppity women.

Most Marxists will probably have a fit about her article. Not only do they know a proper theory when they see one, they know a heretic when they see one as well. (I'll let you know when the inquisition starts.) Darwin and Marx might have made their contribution to overthrowing the 'authority' of the bible but as yet there hasn't been a contender when it comes to overthrowing the 'authority' of Marx . . . he still remains supreme among many . . . Not a word or a phrase can be deviated from. (There should be a book in the way Marx replaced the bible as a source of explanation for creation and the way the world works.) Sometimes I envy them their certainty . . . it must be comfortable to know that there is *only one* way to explain the world and that it is all written down . . . and can be learnt by heart.

How come we haven't had the joy of certainties for years? Upbringing? Disillusionment? Defence? The only certainty I have is that if I am still here tomorrow . . . I will write. It would be better to talk though.

Do hope you have recovered from your dietary/drink disability by the time you receive this. If it's any consolation, the slightest irregularity in my eating/drinking habits has the same results and I don't think that the problem has genetic origins. I also reject the explanations that involve age and poor diet but I could be convinced of a connection between over-indulgence, guilt and rapid elimination by any means. Perhaps we should start keeping records . . . I can just imagine you filling in a chart to record your bodily functions while the post continues to pile up. By the way, you seem to be in danger of letting the post assume unnatural importance in your life. The world will not end if the post remains 'undone'. For a person who managed to overcome the guilty-housewife syndrome, I don't see that effort applied to overcoming the post-problem would be impossible. It can't be hard to rationalize that your time and efforts are better placed elsewhere!

My daily problem is not the post but the children. I think I am on the verge of schizophrenia – brought about by the fast and vast changes in my attitudes towards them. At times I think them delightful examples of healthy young people and at others, I see them as miserable, mean manipulating males. (Good alliteration, eh? Obviously an English teacher inside me somewhere trying to get out!) I worked very late one night during the week and didn't arise at the usual hour to greet the children.

Instead, Jay made the early morning cup of tea (tea bags and butterless toast), organized breakfast for himself and Aaron, packed his lunch and even made an attempt to clean up the kitchen. I was so impressed by the signs of sensitivity, responsibility and maturity that I was stunned by the nine o'clock developments when he reverted to tripping Aaron, calling him a 'spastic' and generally creating havoc. Aaron wandered around complaining that no-one loved him (designed, I'm sure, to bring an immediate response from me) and all I could see were these two, well-trained, 'pro-feminist' males using all the ploys that I consider anti-feminist and awful. I can't help but think that raising male children within a feminist environment just gives them additional ammunition to exploit women. It's almost worth betting (in true Australian style) that all my input and all the effort to make them see that they are responsible for their own shitwork, will end in their scuttling off into the wide world to find a female who will do for them what their mother refused to do on principle. Enough of the children. Why should they disturb me in their absence (they are at school) as well as in their presence?

I was taken, in your last letter, by your comments on current 'living arrangements', and have been doing some research (from the privacy and comfort of my study, of course) by thinking about women and 'living arrangements' here. Either we are, as Australia often is, behind in current trends, or the people I know are in a different category altogether from your circle of friends.

Most women I know are still locked into the servicing role, are resentful of it and are trying to work out ways of dealing with their low self-esteem within the conventional framework of marriage and coupledom (thus the affairs and part-time 'careers'!) I sometimes think that's why several of them are *discouraged* from keeping in touch with me. I'm one of the few who has refused to stay within the acceptable boundaries and no doubt that's fairly threatening – especially to husbands. After all, if I can act as though the boundaries don't exist and without showing the proper respect for established forms, so can their wives!

In a way I envy you your freedom to *choose* your friends according to the life you are living now. Coming back to Australia and the familiar environment has meant coming back to 'old' friends, who, although I have lots of bonds with them, are 'historical accidents' rather than people who share my current values and ideals. Having kids adds a slightly different dimension too. They are happy and untroublesome in the company of other kids and it's easy to become part of a social scene that is based on their needs and interests rather than mine. Here's the trick question for today . . . Is it better to follow my own pursuits with the children irritable and bored (and interrupting) or is it better to take them out and have me irritable and bored . . . you decide and make it your May contribution to their upbringing!

There, I am back to the children again having sworn off them only a few minutes ago.

Back on the 'living arrangements'. It seems to me that the prevalent pattern here is for couples to marry, have kids, divorce and for the men to remarry younger women (remember that old *joke* about men trading in one fifty-year-old for two twenty-five-year-olds?) The women who have been left take their kids (usually at the awkward pre-teen to teenage stage) and move into poverty and discontent, while the men are rejuvenated through their young wives and new, young families. It's a convenient pattern for men – but if there are going to be two women for every male, the supply of women has to run out eventually. Maybe we'll return to a system of 'arranged' marriages where the wealthiest men will be able to 'buy' girl children at birth . . . maybe all the older women will be forced into becoming the service workers, and servants and nannies will come back into fashion. Alternatively, it's possible that medical 'advances' associated with amniocentesis will be used to arrange for sex of children through abortion in order to produce the required number of females – except of course that both men and women still prefer to have male offspring.

The ANZAAS Conference went off as planned – that is with women's studies on the agenda (the last listing on the programme) and with only the committed few feminists turning up to the women's sessions. The paper I did on feminist publishing and the importance of journals to provide the forum for legitimating women's perspective went off reasonably well although I was a little nervous. It's the first time I've done a public performance for quite a while. One of the most interesting sessions was on Women and the Law. It was introduced and chaired by Michael Kirby (do you remember him? He's now Chairman of the Law Reform Commission). There was a paper, or really a 'report', from a female solicitor on the absence of women from high places in Sydney legal firms, with evidence of blatant discrimination which Mr Kirby was reluctant to acknowledge. There was also a report from a barrister (who lectures at the New South Wales Institute of Technology and made me feel good about having applied to do law there) about the difficulties faced by females at 'the bar'. Some funny stories which made the pomp and ceremony of the legal profession look very much like Virginia Woolf's observations in '*Three Guineas*' – men with their uniforms and costumes posturing about their self-importance. It's the same old story. Women are now almost 50 per cent of the ingoing law students (their academic results are better than men's), but there are hardly any women in top positions because of streaming and male nepotism. It's true of medicine too, of course, as well as teaching and other 'professional' areas. Obviously, several of the men at the session saw women's failure to 'reach the top' as women's own problem . . . as though the path were clear and there were no obstructions placed in the way by individual men or by the male-as-norm system. Fifty per cent of student intake *should* result in equal distribution of top positions according to the men – in spite of the evidence that women make up fifty per cent of the population without there being any hint that women should therefore have fifty per cent of the top positions in politics, that there should be equal distribution of power and resources among women and men. Really, I sometimes think that male tunnel-vision must be a genetic disability – (maybe medical science will find a way to operate on it and cut it out – like a lobotomy). Surely no 'thinking' person could listen to the information presented and still insist that men and their system are fair, just, and concerned about equality. It must be genetic!

Still on the law. On Sunday night I spoke to the mother of one of the children at Aaron's school. She is doing the Graduate Law Course at the University of New South Wales and told me that the original thirty-five students (of whom I was not one) had dropped to eighteen and suggested that I contact the Dean there about starting in second semester and picking up the first semester subjects at a later date. I thought it was at least worth talking to the Dean and rang his office. His secretary told me that I should ring the Executive secretary of the Faculty but that I couldn't do so because she was away sick. I rang anyway to leave a message and found she was not sick but that she could not help me, and I should ring the Administrative Secretary – except that she was away, sick. With tongue-in-cheek, I tried again and found that the Administrative Secretary was away but that her secretary recommended that I contact the Dean. Full circle and shades of the Australian concept of eventually disappearing up one's own rear orifice.

I do like the idea of your doing a review of your own writing – in anticipation of the inevitable criticism that will come your way. Could you just leave it as a reference in one of your books (the '*Letters*'?) which you can be assured that few reviewers will read from cover to cover, and then you could have the pleasure of accusing the critics of plagiarism as well as vindictiveness? It appeals to me far more to have the last laugh. I think there must be a nasty streak in me somewhere.

I must go and attend to some chores. My feet are cold and a walk to the post office and the shops is the quickest way to warm them. I had forgotten that even in Australia, feet can become cold. I used to chuckle at the English and the Canadians who were constantly trying to monitor and avoid draughts, but I find that I too am running around looking for signs of cold air. I suppose it's a slight improvement on the committed search for dust and dirt, although I wouldn't like to have to defend that in an argument . . . in the sum total of human affairs and all that. Hope that summer has come to London and that I can at least take comfort in the knowledge that you have warm feet. . . .

It's such a beautiful morning it is difficult to believe. The sun is streaming in through the study window and it is an incredible twenty-two degrees even at this early hour (eight a.m.) – I have just turned off the central heating! I suppose the English will think it is a heatwave . . . and all go down like flies. (I assume that *is* an Australian expression.)

Understandably, this rare glimpse of the sun makes me feel good but it is not the only contributing factor. I have been reading some of Rebecca West's early journalism (1911–15) and have been inspired by her acid prose and acerbic wit. I truly didn't know that women had been so outrageous in print before . . . it is wonderful. But if I am not careful my present euphoria will give way to depression because I too am trying to make my own contribution to journalism and I suffer enormously by comparison.

It is not just that I couldn't possibly match the wit and the wilyness of Rebecca – but that I assuredly would not be published even if I did a faint imitation. There goes another myth about progress.

While I was reading some of Rebecca's articles it occurred to me that she too probably wouldn't be able to get them published today . . . and not because they are no longer relevant but because they are too close to the bone.

I'm seriously thinking of asking her whether we can type up

one of her articles from 1911 and submit it (under a pseudonym of course) to one of the major papers today. Since those somewhat obscure stories of Virginia Woolf's were submitted to a feminist publisher as a 'joke' . . . and were rejected, I have no faith whatsoever in the belief that the true quality of the 'artist' is recognised by editors. As you have so competently demonstrated in your book on publishing (I wish I could review your book, under a pseudonym of course . . . what fun), rationality is not the underlying force in the publishing world. If today's established editors rejected Rebecca, it would be some good additional material for you . . . and some good documentation for my thesis that rather than consolidate their gains, every fifty years women have to begin again from scratch. Only loser would be Rebecca . . . perhaps we had better give it a miss.

How is the journalism going? Did I tell you about my little episode with one of our national papers which wanted to do 'a few things on women'? After talking to the editor, it struck me that the very last thing they want from a feminist is a convincing case.

It took me some time to figure this out, (I know, slow learner – think how long it took me to learn I wasn't happily married!). I made some suggestions for articles – what happens when women are interviewed by men, what criticisms are made of women's books, how women (apart from Mrs Thatcher) aren't taken seriously – and I backed them all up with my research findings. Then she said that they simply weren't controversial enough topics for articles, and that they would not bring in letters to the editor (evidently the sign of success) and so they simply wouldn't do.

And that was when it hit me. Why would an editor want an article from a feminist which was reasonable, accurate, and proved the point? Feminism has to be absurd, readily mockable and then all the readers can write in and say they don't want any more of that silly women's lib stuff.

The editor didn't want a *good* feminist article, she wanted a *bad* one, so that the world could go on its self righteous way with nothing challenged and could continue to scoff at those crazy women who never know when to stop.

I said I would like to do an article on being a troublemaker at the British Museum – having recently had first-hand experience of this role in my research for '*Women of Ideas*'. All the books I wanted to consult were by women, and we all know where the books on women are kept. In the depots. Women are the minor writers and stored. So books written by women have to be ordered in advance as they are not readily available 'on the shelves'. Putting in my order every day (in advance) for books to be delivered I was cryptically asked on one occasion whether I took pleasure in being perverse!

You could write a really good article on that. That's the problem of course. That's why the idea was rejected. Who could possibly disagree with you, the editor asked me gravely?

And then she wanted to know what topics *I hadn't* done any research on and went on to suggest a whole range of puerile possibilities, which if I had taken up, would have admirably suited her purpose and exposed me as a ridiculous woman with a bee in my bonnet, (and not the rational, responsible, reserved and reliable person I really am, of course.)

Feminism is a 'set-up' for such editors, a humorous diversion, a scapegoat to get the readers in. I suppose I shouldn't be surprised by this having just written 500 pages on the same topic for '*Women of Ideas*', but it does still come as something of a shock to the sytem to find that you are required for well-planned entertainment value and that the editor would see it as a failure if you were to be taken seriously. No wonder she was antagonistic to my suggestion to write an article on why and how women are not taken seriously.

Maybe I should write an article on sexual harassment by editors . . . because that is what it is. I'm sure men aren't subjected to the same pressure to be silly . . . in print (come to think of it, I could be wrong on that; think of what some men have written . . . Freud for example).

Anna is always a source of sound advice on the media . . . Perhaps I had better ask her about some of the tricks of the trade. We had a marvellous talk during the week about the project she wants to do next. She says it comes from reading the chapters on The Logic of Dominance in '*Invisible Women*' but I hadn't thought about it before. She wants to do something on the politics of male resistance, and some of her ideas and material are superb. Instead of simply stating – as I am often prone to do – that little has changed over the last few centuries, Anna wants to show that the absence of progress isn't some mysterious accident . . . or even the failure of women to get themselves organised . . . but that it is because men *obstruct* it; she wants to put the onus on men, not women or the fates. Simple, safe and sure . . . and good feminism; politically sound, ethical from the point of view of women . . . so could even be classed as 'correct'.

She has masses of evidence from all sorts of institutions and agencies which demonstrate that men have done many things to keep women's values and priorities from being taken seriously and becoming a major focus. In some ways, it is an extension of the line I adopted about women's education . . . that it has been more a case of men trying to defend their privileges and keep women out, than of women trying to make gains. It focuses on male behaviour as problematic, puts men and their values and strategies under the microscope instead of assuming that their behaviour is either the norm or beyond reproach. (Of course she will no doubt get some of the shit that I do . . . or that Liz Stanley does . . . and be accused of concentrating her attention on *men* and thereby falling into another sexist trap; I agree that that is a possible danger but that it is even more dangerous not to study 'the enemy'.)

I don't think Anna will go as far as Berit Ås (the Norwegian feminist philosopher) who maintains that every time women get close to realising their aspirations, men have a war, a recession or a revolution, in order to insist that feminism is a luxury and one that can no longer be afforded.

I have always thought that Berit's theory makes quite a lot of sense; you can see it again now with the war and the recession . . . 'We have these really important male issues to think about and it would be nice to think about equality, equal pay, and sex discrimination . . . but at the moment there are "our boys" risking death, and our breadwinners demoralised . . . and we have to get these problems of men sorted out first and maybe then we can think about creches, and more women in parliament and even take a closer look at the ever-growing gap between the pay of women and men . . .' All you need to do really, to substantiate Berit's thesis, is to start with the chicken rather than the egg when it comes to looking at history . . . and besides, the outrageousness of her position has always appealed to me.

I think Anna will be more subtle, and in the end, probably more subversive. She thinks men have been engaged in a campaign of passive resistance (and the choice of the word 'passive' for the ostensibly 'active' male sex will in itself be an affront to many), and that they have cunningly avoided open confrontation – and accusations of sexism – by opting for the 'penis-power-ploy' of professing their sympathy with feminist aims and ideals. They couldn't agree more that women have genuine ideals. They couldn't agree more that women have genuine grievances, that there is no justice, and that patriarchy is a disgrace . . .

And then they do nothing!

This really leaves women in a difficult position. They can be disarmed by male support and approval, and they can find that the enemy has evaporated . . . but *nothing has changed*. Really, it is quite applicable to what you were saying about women's position in the legal profession. Those men at the ANZAAS Conference – if look at it through Anna's lens – were passively resisting women's entry by their reliance on reason and 'fair play' . . . You know the old stand 'It's all open to women and we can't help it if the women don't take up the opportunities' (a common stance in engineering and the sciences) and 'Really, we would love to appoint a women to the job . . . if only we could find one who was truly qualified'. I like Anna's approach; instead of getting exasperated, and thinking that we are not explaining ourselves adequately, or organising ourselves efficiently, we can start saying we *could* do it if only men were not so petty and didn't do so much to *stop* us. Neat twist eh?

If you look at women's history you can see that this understanding about the obstructionism and resistance of men isn't all that new . . . but who knows about women's history? Understandably, it is a closely guarded secret. But Christabel Pankhurst knew a lot about the passive resistance of males even though she called it by another name. She knew that for almost sixty years women had been seeking the vote and had been assured by many (changing) male politicians that their case was reasonable and the reform would prevail . . . soon. And nothing changed. Women were no closer to getting the vote after sixty years of struggle, than they had been at the beginning. And she certainly didn't think it was women's fault.

Christabel wouldn't let men get away with passive resistance. She forced them into the open, she promoted confrontation, so that the enemy was clearly identified. Maybe Anna will conclude that we have to revive militancy if we are going to get anywhere. Must say I won't object . . . although I don't know about going to jail. Hunger striking probably wouldn't do me any harm at the moment though . . . I still haven't lost that Australian weight.

I wish I had written up the chapter on Hazel Hunkins Hallinan for, *'There's Always Been a Women's Movement'*. She talked to me about the passive resistance of males early this century and how and why the women's Congressional Union was formed, (with Alice Paul, Lucy Burns, Crystal Eastman and Mary Beard among its members . . . that was a society I wouldn't have minded joining). For years the women had worked to get the suffrage amendment included in the platform of the Democrats, and they were often successful. But then when the Democrats came to power . . . the amendment somehow magically disappeared. And all that energy and effort was just wasted. I'd love to be able to give Anna the typescript of it but at the moment all I have are Hazel's words and they could be on *any* one of the six tapes I made with her . . . and I can't lend Anna the tapes because it is possible, by some unimagined stroke of good fortune that in the next few days I might find the occasional hours to get down and start writing. (I'm praying to the goddess for good fortune, but also trying to do something about it!)

I was telling Anna about our 'loving husbands' theory and she thought it delightful. It is really the 'private' version of the 'public' strategy isn't it? And Charlotte Perkins Gilman knew all about it . . . as does Dora Russell. Husbands who proclaim to be all for women's rights, who think only of the welfare of their wives – and who are thereby successful in pre-empting any change. (Actually, the more I think about it, the more I am inclined to the view that it has been males who have been the manipulative sex . . . presenting themselves in a positive and flattering light while at the same time ensuring that their power base is not eroded.)

Anna and I started an inventory of 'What about So-and So?' (aren't I kind, not mentioning names?), and we decided that even with the most supportive males we know . . . even the ones who call themselves 'committed feminists' (I prefer to call them 'bearded feminists'), we can detect the operation of passive resistance, and the strategies for obstructing change. Certainly started to think of some of the male supporters of women in a slightly new light after our consciousness raising activity.

Then we got onto *my* writing and Anna started to ask me some probing questions which I didn't want to answer. Like you, she said that I was making a phobia out of the post (but neither of you *see* it each day when it is delivered!) I did agree though that my priorities were wrong, that I should be doing the writing *first* and then fitting the post in afterwards, and not the other way round. The thing is that as no-one else is dependent on the writing, I don't feel guilty when it isn't done, but I *do* feel guilty when the post isn't done! It is my guilt factor that is determining my behaviour. After Anna had been and done her 'bit', I decided that writing comes first!

But to do it I had to get everything in order which included filing what I couldn't throw out . . . (and there were thirteen garbage bags full of waste paper . . . where were you? You know how much I hate emptying the garbage and how you have always done that as the concession to my peculiarities). I filed quite a bit but the pile that was proving difficult got shoved in a cupboard . . . thanks to your advice on adopting the same attitude to the post as the housework; I reckon that by the time I get round to rediscovering the cupboard pile, there is every likelihood that the contents will be beyond the recommended date for use!

All I had left to do was to re-sort my books . . . they bore no resemblance to alphabetical order after I finished '*Women of Ideas*', and I simply can't bear not to be able to find a book when I need it. And finish '*Feminist Theorists*'.

It's not so easy to get it out of the way though. I am still waiting on replies from quite a few contributors about queries on their articles. Mainly it was the references . . . although a couple of times I nearly went bananas . . . like the name of one man spelt five different ways in three pages . . . how on earth do you know which one to choose? But in the next few days I should be able to finalise it and send it off for typesetting. That will be a relief. It has worried me having that hanging over me. It should have been finished before now.

And then all I will have to do is the proofs and the index . . . they should come through the dreaded *post* anytime now.

But I know I am inefficient and easily distracted sometimes. Yesterday the final version of Ann's article on Charlotte Perkins Gilman arrived and I was delighted with it. But I noticed as I went through it that she made no distinction between Gilman's fiction and non-fiction writing. That's a pretty unusual departure. For example, only very rarely have I seen the fiction of Virginia Woolf used in the same way as her non-fiction . . . like '*A Room of One's Own*' and '*Three Guineas*' . . . to illuminate her life, without reference to the fact that one is 'fact' and the other 'fiction'. And I got all caught up in thinking (and jotting down things) about the boundary line betweeen fact and fiction, between reality and fantasy . . . you know how intrigued I am by these issues.

In the case of Gilman, Ann implied that her non-fiction was really an assessment of life as it *is* under patriarchy whereas her fiction is more about life as it *could be* (like '*Herland*'). But then what do you do with '*The Yellow Wallpaper*' which is really a fictional account of how it is?

What absurd boundary lines we create . . . they don't work at all.

When I was making some notes I kept coming back to some of the conversations I had with Jay. Do you remember that time I had a dream that he cut a hole in my *only* pair of purple jeans and I told him in the morning that every time I looked at him, all I could think of was that he had deliberately destroyed my *only* pair of purple jeans; that I was cross with him and he had better keep out of my sight for the day? We had some metaphysical discussions after that on the basis of *after* the event, when all you have is *memory*, does it matter whether it is a memory of something that *really happened* (and goddess, what does that mean?) or the memory of something that you *dreamed*? I can remember that he finally decided that the dividing lines were blurred and instead of arguing that it was just a dream, changed his tack and started the 'But Dale, it was only a pair of jeans' line and that I 'could always get another pair', so it wasn't really worth me being upset about it.

I know I made dad furious once when we were discussing some event of my childhood and I gave *my* version of what had happened, and then he gave *his* . . . and of course never the two would match. And I said that for me the *truth* was contained in my version and that nothing he could say would alter that, that for years I had lived my life on the basis of that *truth* and that it was now part of my fabric. And for dad of course I was basing my values on something that *didn't happen*, something that was a lie.

I know there is no danger that I will ever forget that people construct their own reality, that human beings are not led to the same version of events and of the world by the same physical evidence. But I am still puzzled about *how* people come to make sense of the world in their various ways. And even Freud said dreams make a difference, and the way we recall our childhood makes a difference. All the things that go into the melting pot of our personal view of the world, and the way we make sense of it; yet we know so little about it. As Dora (Russell) says, we can put a man on the moon but we have no more idea than Aristotle . . . and possibly even less . . . as to why people think and act as they do.

Yet all this is so crucial for feminism. I don't know why the apparently same set of circumstances will make one woman a fighter, a protester and a feminist, and another cling even more tenaciously to convention. I don't know how or why people change, and without that notion, how can you even begin to 'get the message across' as so many so elegantly phrase it? I can't talk to a women's studies class as I talk to Jay (more's the pity) and discuss the issue of a destroyed pair of purple jeans. Still, I suppose I am being a bit of a pessimist; at least some things are predictable.

Not so long ago Lizzie and I were in a lift talking about sexual harassment when a young woman got in and was quickly pursued by a young man who 'grabbed' her and used a considerable amount of force. Well, Amazons to the rescue, wasn't it? I mean we were even in the right psychological state. Between the two of us and within seconds, we had removed him from the girl and the lift, and were preparing ourselves for a grateful response, when she started to cry, and loudly demanded, 'What did you do that for? He's my boyfriend. Why did you do that you rotten things, he might never speak to me again, now!'

There was no alternative. We took the lift down again and picked him up, (I must say he still looked rather stunned). We attached them and removed ourselves. Moral of the story – what looks like *sexual harassment* to us could well look like *true love* to someone else.

And it is no solution whatsoever to say one is right and the other wrong. It is that we start from different premises, that we have different assumptions and proceed to make sense of the world in different ways. I'd always argue that both points of view are equally *valid* . . . that to the young woman true love (and his demonstration of it) was no less real than was our view of sexual harassment. But I wouldn't argue that both are equally useful or justifiable.

Back to the world of Bertrand Russell (I'll never be able to hold my head up again as a true feminist); you can prove anything, it simply depends on the assumptions you begin with . . . so the issue is *which assumption?* I like my feminist ones, they have been more helpful than any others, they make me feel better, and besides, I think they are morally justifiable.

But they are absolutely no help whatsoever when it comes to working out what is fact and what is fiction.

A bloody male like Samuel Pepys can write his diary and it can become one of the most authoritative and 'factual' historical sources. Elizabeth Robins can build a narrative around verbatim speeches delivered by Christabel Pankhurst and it is called an imaginative indulgence. I don't even know what these damned letters of ours are . . . yes they are 'fact' in that they are taken from our daily correspondence but there has been quite a lot of fiction go into them too . . . as we think of the possibility of libel, the risk of upsetting mother (and other friends) and as we 'reconstruct' them now . . . after the event.

If there is no truth (and I for one cannot find any truth other than the absolute one that I will die one day . . . probably), then there can be no falsity; if there is no one reality, then what a load of rubbish is the idea of fantasy? If *'Man Made Language'* and *'Intruders on the Rights of Men'* are not truth, but simply our version (and damned good versions they are too), then what is fiction? I used to think it was an insult when some people (who shall remain nameless) said that my research was fiction . . . but now I think they were 'right'. There is nothing else it could be.

Maybe we should launch a new series . . . 'Darwin – a fiction', or 'Freud – a fantasy.' I'll have trouble with Ted on that one though . . . he keeps saying Newton is different.

We almost came to blows the other night . . . I suppose it was a result of my jottings on this problem. I was certainly looking for discussion but as you know, I have never looked for a fight. I am heartily sick of the great god Newton and his invention, *Gravity*. As far as I am concerned, it is a name for something that is inexplicable, a pretty poetic concept for something that is not comprehensible to *Man*. To me, it looks suspiciously like another word for Jehovah or God, a sort of first cause . . . where it all began. I simply cannot believe that scientists expect me to take them seriously when they talk about this powerful force which exists in the middle of the earth and pulls us all towards it. And keeps us upright. Even the medieval mystics had a better story than that.

Strange though, whenever I suggest that they go back to the drawing board and try again, I am greeted by outrage. Again, a bit like other 'set' theories that can't be changed . . . Marxism, Newtonism or Freudianism . . . either you go along with them, or you are an heretic. The goddess preserve feminism from such a fate.

Have you come to the conclusion yet that I would be better writing my book than speculating on the nature of the universe? I have. Still, where else is one permitted to discuss these things? Mary Astell said in the late seventeenth century that she was turned on by ideas (she was influenced by another man, Descartes – now he really fascinates me), but after her it seems to have gone out of fashion. When I was asked recently how I explained my entry to feminism, I wasn't taken seriously when I said intellectual curiosity. In future I shall stick to our strategy of attributing all credit to our state school upbringing. Don't suppose that I can get a less favourable response if I insist that everything I am today, I owe to Burwood Girls' High School. (But will it bring an end to private schooling?)

By the way, I just *loved* your reference to the reviews. If we can fit it in, I should do a review in '*Sisters*' for, as you say, no prestigious reviewer will ever read it from cover to cover (and only a prestigious reviewer would be on to the patronising 'superficiality' and 'hastily written' approach); the form is so predictable that there is every chance that I could do an accurate piece . . . and then sue them for plagiarism as you suggest. (That's another strand of the law you could specialise in . . . think what women could do if they started to take men to court for stealing women's ideas . . . we could block the whole system.)

There might be something in it for promotion as well. I have already said that '*Sisters*' should try and be a commercial proposition and have justified it on the grounds that child-minders are expensive and that if you are going to finish your law degree, write your books and stay sane (as well as stay on good terms with mother who will soon lose her enthusiasm for her grandchildren if she is obliged to spend more than a day a week with them), then we need money. I even suggested the other day that we might be a much greater commercial success with a different title for the book. '*Dialogue Between Sisters*' sounds terribly tame. What about '*Sensational Exposé of Secret Lives of Incestuous Lesbians*'? We could sell a million then.

With an introduction from mum, along with her blessing, we could have all the suburban dinner party circuits convinced that they had always been right . . . and we had always been terrible. It's almost worth it for the sanctimonious sympathy mum would no doubt receive.

❧ Coogee, June 1982

I am afraid that your idea of our becoming journalists when we grow up has just received a crushing blow! This morning's mail brought me back my carefully prepared and promptly written article on women and publishing with a note stating that my 'allegations' were not sufficiently substantiated. Presumably I was to quote more publishing personalities than I did and base my argument on what *other* people have said rather than what I have discovered or thought. And in a way, I should have known that would be the case. Apart from the irony of writing an article on why women don't get published – and expecting to have it published, I should have realized that articles, like reviews, are not meant to be accurate or insightful portrayals of issues or events. They are meant to attract attention and sell more papers. Familiar and famous names from the publishing world are far more marketable than serious considerations of who gets published and why – written by *Ms. Nobody*. Even so, I feel a bit disheartened and wish you were here to say 'of course' – and to share a bottle of wine.

I do, however, have some good news. I have been accepted into the Law Course at the New South Wales Institute of Technology and start lectures at the end of July. They will, I am sure, coincide exactly with my tutorials for the MA in Women's Studies at the University of NSW and I will have a hell of a time juggling the two and fitting in everything else. It is *verboten* for students here to be enrolled at two different institutes or to study two different courses at the one time. I shall have to be careful . . . but at 35, I can't afford the time to finish one before starting the other. Not that I am so interested in having another MA after my name (M.A.M.A. looks a bit silly), but I would like to finish the Women's Studies course. While I know that an MA in Women's Studies is hardly the most marketable degree around at the moment (it's referred to by 'proper' academics as a 'Mickey Mouse' degree), I am sure it will come in handy in the future.

*Loving husbands, eh? A form of passive resistance? It makes such a lot of sense. I applied the formula to the women I know who live with understanding men (there aren't that many of them) and it's true that they are prevented from 'going too far' by a sense of fair play and gratitude to their men for being so well-informed and sympathetic. How could you, after all, be critical of a man who expects you to perform as his 'wife' at a business function when he has just gone to the trouble of reading the latest Women's Press publication in order to understand you better? It's like being grateful to men for exhibiting just a slightly greater degree of understanding than that shown by the meanest and most pusillanimous little man. Like . . . She practically has an orgasm in gratitude to her husband when he condescends to wipe up after dinner *and* after she has worked, shopped, prepared dinner, cleared up and washed up. 'He's wonderful . . . Despite the fact that he *could* just sit back and read the newspaper . . .' Loving husbands, eh?

I was delighted to learn that you had finally come to terms with the post (on one occasion, at least) and had dealt with it sensibly. Not that I can afford to be wise and sanctimonious. . . I still have two of my pregnancy outfits hanging in the wardrobe, four years after sterilization. Why don't I throw them out, get rid of them? I'm not sure whether it's a middle-class hang-up . . . 'there's a lot of good material in them' – or whether it's a more

---

* There will be a book forthcoming. '*Loving Husbands: Can We Afford Them?*' by Lynne Spender and Dale Spender.

sinister notion of reminding myself of the past. Either way, I can't seem to throw them out. Hopefully, a moth will get at them but then I'll be upset that I didn't give them to someone who could have used them. There, you see . . . it must be the 'waste-not-want-not' hang-up. It has nothing to do with symbolism and motherhood and guilt . . . I think it's an issue that I do not want to explore in depth.

I'd much rather talk about the fiction/non-fiction division that you raised (which I thoroughly enjoyed and have thought about a great deal). It arrived on my intellectual doorstep in another form. I was re-reading Jessie Bernard's '*The Future of Marriage*' (I am *still* trying to write that book on marriage) and came across the reference to there being two marriages within every marriage – his and hers – and that his is always better than hers! What is fact and fiction there? It seems that men's facts are so often fictional to women (and vice versa) that the line between the two is merely a matter of who has the power to enforce their view . . . and usually it is men. If it comes to whether or not women and children are going to eat and have a roof over their heads, who are we to argue that our female reality is more real than men's money? What I want to know is how we can manage to have our own money so that the fact/fiction dichotomy can be worked out on a basis other than power. Do you have any answers?

Talking of women and children, I was stunned at the weekend by a woman, whom I had considered a 'like-minded' feminist, expressing displeasure and even distaste at my delight in the concept of child-*free* rather than child*less* women. Raised the whole issue of whether or not motherhood and reproduction etc. is a disability or a form of power.

I suppose it depends on which reality you adopt. Certainly I agree that it *should* be a source of power and I have no trouble visualising a time in the past when birthing and women's biological cycles were the only 'truths' that people had. Can you imagine what men must have felt and thought (remember Aziza raising this at the American Women's Studies Conference in Indiana?) when they saw that women bled – regularly and in tune with the moon and tides – and didn't die? Or when they saw women reproduce themselves and feed their offspring from their own bodies? Magic! Enough to send men scurrying off to form secret societies (which became men's clubs, then councils and then governments) and to make up complex rules and regulations (laws) which gave them some sort of power and a sense of importance. They must have put so much energy into convincing themselves that their appendages were more than 'toys for the boys'. An explanation perhaps for those cultures that revered the 'flip-flop phallus' rather than women's life-giving powers . . . so what's so different about our culture?

I'm afraid I can't see much future in women merely asserting that society *should* elevate reproduction and motherhood to a higher plane and accord them greater status. Societies organized by men are based on devaluing or ignoring women's contributions and not on happily moving over to make room for them. I am quite convinced that medical 'advances' like test-tube babies and artificial insemination by donor are the early stages of a bigger move to take reproduction right away from women. Then we won't have even a potential source of power.

But where does that leave us? If we continue to have children in a society where no allowances (like child-care) are made to permit us easily to do anything other than have and raise kids, then the possibilities for change in women's favour are almost non-existent. You know the old saying – 'Keep them barefoot, pregnant and in the kitchen' – they can't do much from there. Yet if we decide not to have children, then we end up being no different from men – but still without any power – and that is hardly what the struggle is all about.

I think instead, I'll start a campaign to convince women that they should cease being sexually available to men. It might even take on. Think what a source of relief it might be to all those women who currently have to go through the motions of having headaches, periods, or of feigning deep sleep, in order to control men's self-indulgent sexual appetites. You know, I have always said that women's sexual appetites (or lack thereof) are the best natural contraceptive that there is. If I could convince women that refusal to meet men's sexual demands was essential to the ultimate survival of the species, women could feel good about saying 'no' instead of feeling guilty that the poor little pets might burst. I suppose what would actually happen would be an increase in wife-beating and rape . . . would the immediate loss of proof of sexual potency upset men more than the long term loss of sons in their own images?

I have a lot of thinking to do on this issue!!!!

Meanwhile, I have to turn my attention to working out new strategies for dealing with the two small males with whom I have daily contact. I'm afraid my liberal attitudes and philosophical child-rearing theories sometimes backfire. My motherly advice to the larger of the two small persons was met last night with an accusation that I seemed to forget that 'children are people too!' The hide of him! I taught him that in a context where *I* was the friend and *we* were dealing with a common *foe*, and now he has the audacity to use it against me. And justifiably so. I was laying down the law without even pretending to consult him . . . can see some awkward situations arising out of this. I can also see, as we have discussed before, that he will use his insights into feminism *against* women rather than *for* them, when his interests are at stake. It makes me realize that the only reason I really want to earn any money over and above *my* minimal requirements is to send them both off to boarding school, so that I can theorize without interruption and can blame the school for the children's failure to fit in with my theories. For the moment though, I shall have to leave here and take up with *them* . . .

V-DAY   V-DAY   V-DAY   V-DAY   V-DAY

The only one I have ever witnessed. Union Jacks flying through-out the town. 'An operation boldly planned, bravely fought, and brilliantly something . . .' (Mrs Thatcher in the Commons . . . first prize for alliteration anyway.) They declared the day – Falkland Islands Liberation Day, and the British are *not* going to sell the *Invincible* to the Australians after all. The taste of glory has been too much . . . they think they will probably need the ship again . . . next time the Tories' popularity is on the wane. So far the whole war has been a huge success . . . and all done for people who only recently were ruled to be *non*-British; *and all done without rationing* . . . (much disappointment on that score I think. No-one over here convinced it was the *real* thing without ration-ing.) *Obscene*!

What with Victory and the World Cup, our television – raised on good feminist principles – has gone on the blink!

In case you think that this is all that is happening in my life, let me tell you that I am also concerned with the *real* world and am up to my ears in proofs. It is a strange feeling getting it all back typeset ('*Women of Ideas*'). Of course I know that typesetters are entrusted with the magic task of converting my personal beliefs into truth with their technology, but I am still impressed by the magic.

It all look so different when it is in *print*. It bears little resemblance to the way it leaves here, to the way I write to you. I must admit to astonishment when I make myself acknowledge that everything in it, I *made up*, and here it is, transformed into 'authority'. Maybe I just lack confidence . . . or maybe this is a phenomenon that needs further examination. Do you think there could be a book in it?*

Reading through it, I have regrets of course . . . the prime one being that the damned thing is so long, and will take so long to proof read. And there are also the embarrassing moments when I come across something that jars, that clashes and sends me into a state of hot flushes. A couple of times I have thought, 'My goodness, how awful' but basically it has been over the style . . . (can you see the 1983 review . . . 'Obviously in her rush to deliver so many books, Dale Spender does not leave herself time to revise, otherwise she would have noted the contortions of some of her sentences . . . and changed them.' Two answers of course . . . one that George Sand never revised anything . . . and the other that I *do* revise but I lack concentration. I certainly lack concentration in doing these proofs . . . goddess it is a dreary job checking every word.)

There have been a few surprises. There were a couple of things that I didn't know that I knew . . . and that really makes me feel a bit of a dunce. There is that perfectly ridiculous situation when I get engrossed in what I am reading and find myself thinking, 'Goodness me, isn't that interesting . . . *I didn't know that . . .*' I just hope no-one can read my thoughts . . . obviously if I wrote it, I have to *know* it. Evidence of more magic perhaps, or an indication that it is fiction . . . or maybe just the sheer potential of language to be all things to the same woman.

Anyhow, there is little in terms of substance that I would want to change . . . although that doesn't alter the persistent conviction that I would do it so much better if I were writing it *now*. Sometimes I wish the touch were a bit lighter . . . I don't like the heavy stuff and try so hard to ensure that I avoid it, but there are still the occasional 'purple patches' I am afraid.

---

* Satirical reference to the fact that this is the substance of Lynne's book *'Intruders on the rights of men: Women's unpublished heritage'*.

Evidently it is not just in my book that I fall short of the desired standard of 'light and witty' though. You say that the newspaper rejected your article because it was not sufficiently substantial . . . well *mine was also rejected because it was not sufficiently humorous.* Now what do you think that means?

It could mean that we are both miserable failures but on the grounds of 'politically incorrect', I rule out that possibility. Keeping in mind the title of that superb Swedish book, *'Don't Cry: Do Research'*! what other alternative explanations are there? A little 'research' on the issue wouldn't go astray.

Hypothesis: (common to feminism over the last few centuries). *No matter what women do it is wrong and will be used as a reason for discrediting them.* (Same hypothesis put forward by Mary Astell, 'Sophia', Catherine Macaulay, Mary Wollstonecraft, Christabel Pankhurst and Simone de Beauvoir . . . among others, but having just read the sections on them in *'Women of Ideas'*, they come instantly to mind.)

Experiment: Two women writers with similar background shared assumptions and comparable style, (we have to keep this a controlled experiment of course), each write a piece for national newspapers on two different continents.

Results: One gets rejected because it is not sufficiently serious, and the other because it is not sufficiently funny.

Conclusion: No matter what women do, it is not good enough. It is 'wrong'.

Discussion: It is therefore necessary for all women to be feminists and to understand the implications of the patriarchal assumption, that no matter what women do it is wrong. By the same token, it is absolutely essential that the patriarchal world continues to function along its present lines or else there will be no reason for women to be feminists . . . and we will be out of business.

Therefore . . . just in case you are wondering, be grateful for small mercies and write to the editors expressing our appreciation for their willingness to uphold their end of the patriarchal system. Take consolation in the fact that the world is a meaningful place after all . . . if you think about it in terms of perversity.

Hope that makes you feel better . . . although you shouldn't really need any cheering up; getting into law should have been enough for one week. I am so pleased. My only worry is how on earth are you going to manage it? It was bad enough trying to explain your hectic life to people when it consisted of two kids, one degree, and writing a book, but now that it is *two* degrees, I am sure to be at a loss when asked your reasons. If I say you see yourself as a late starter and you are trying to make up lost ground, I won't be saying anything new . . . it is what I have said about myself at times in relation to my own hectic life? At least people will think it runs in the family and that we are all *slow learners*. Personally, I think mum and dad must take much of the blame . . . they don't even think there is anything strange about the hours we work because they have worked them for so many years.

What will happen when you pass both courses? You probably won't even to able to tell anyone because what you are doing is illegal . . . I think you should be careful on that score, for if I remember rightly, the fact that you are enrolled in another course can be sufficient reason for disqualification from *both*, without reference to your performance in either of them. What does appeal to me is the *distinct* possibility that you will do outstandingly well in both.

You know I have always argued that men's education isn't difficult (and that feminism is the *real* intellectual challenge) but I have always lacked the evidence, the 'hard data' to back up such a claim. Get distinctions in both Lynne, and then we can 'prove' that it isn't difficult to pass their precious tests!

The real intellectual challenge in my life at the moment is the index for '*Women of Ideas*'. It was one thing to recognise that conventional indexes make women's experience and priorities invisible, but quite another to work out a new conceptualisation. I've been going barmy just trying to work out what the categories for the index could be, and haven't even begun to match categories with page numbers. I don't think I can begin to explain what a mammoth job it is and while there is an enormous amount of fun in it, at times (as I think up ways of naming from women's perspective) it is wearying work. Anne is helping me do it. I sit and read out categories to her from every page and she keeps index cards . . . which periodically we have to reshuffle. So far we have been through 800 of the bloody things (index cards) and the physical task itself is almost unmanageable. But do we have some superb categories.

We have put in the entry 'loving husbands' and along with it, 'Radical men' and then have listed Bertrand Russell and John Stuart Mill for example, and have also cross-referenced them with 'champions of women's rights'. The male heroes of the women's movement are certainly going to be seen in a different light.

We have had to invent names . . . like, for example, historically one of the issues women have protested against most vigorously is the arrogant male presumption that a women isn't complete without a man. It is a basic thesis of Cicely Hamilton's book ('*Marriage as a Trade*') and yet, in 'standard' terms, there would be no way of entering *that* particular concept in the index. So we now have 'Completion complex, that is, the incompleteness of a woman without a man' and the references then are to the ridiculous nature of such a concept.

One big entry will be 'Disagreeable women' and of course it will contain references to most of my favourites . . . who were all thoroughly disagreeable (on the grounds that if you were going to be condemned anyway, if you were wrong before you began, then you may as well enjoy what you were doing and really make men uncomfortable). By far the biggest entry though, is 'Harassment' – as far as I can determine at this stage, there must be a reference on every page . . . maybe the book should have just been called '*Harassment*'. Not a jazzy enough title though, is it!

We have fiddled with some of the patriarchal assumptions – the heading 'Economics' is immediately followed by 'Female, (sexual economics)' and contains the sub-headings 'Failure to get a man, lucky to get a man, trading one's person (marriage and prostitution)'. The final sub-heading is 'Economics, male'. How do you like that? Women will not have seen their view of the world displayed so explicitly before and I hope it gives validation to women's experience. Anne and I have enjoyed ourselves when we have been able to forget the hard work . . . both of us get backache and eye strain. It has been a scintillating consciousness-raising experience for me and an exercise in what it *could* be like if women were declaring what was important and what was not.

Obviously, it isn't perfect, but it is a start and it is a practical way of saying that we don't have to accept the classification system that men have devised. The only trouble is that having started on this train of thought, I am likely to continue to devise new categories . . . *long after the index has been typeset*, and I suppose for the next few months (anyway), I'll keep thinking of what I *should* have put in, but didn't think of at the time. Have you got any suggestions for entries?

(And just for the record, I discovered some mistakes that I had made in the book when I had to proof read it, so I added another entry 'mistakes, author's' . . . don't suppose that one has featured too prominently before). Maybe I kid myself . . . it's quite possible that the index might not even be consulted . . . by women readers or reviewers. I can imagine a few reviewers though who would go bonkers . . . I have deliberately refrained from indexing any men who are mentioned in the text on the grounds that what is good for the gander is good for the goose . . . how many indexes in books written by men make women invisible?

But I need a bit of a break from '*Women of Ideas*'. If I'm not careful it will consume my whole life at the moment . . . and that isn't the most efficient way of doing either the proofs or devising the index. Partly because I recognised that it was essential that I give myself some other task that was completely different, (a change being as good as a holiday), I have finally got myself sorted out to begin writing up my 'old ladies'. I've started on Rebecca and found it superbly stimulating. I have drafted out the chapter but at the moment I am not happy with the arrangement. I have done it chronologically and it doesn't work . . . partly because the material I have on her is so uneven. I have much on her early life, and quite a bit on the last few years . . . but as she is 90 it leaves quite a gap in the middle as you can imagine. I am going to have to find a way of writing it up that doesn't make it quite so obvious that there are quite a few silent years in between.

Going back to some of Rebecca's and Dora's ideas about marriage and motherhood was fascinating after your comments on the difference between child*less* and child-*free*; I'm pretty sure Dora would subscribe to the child*less* version and Rebecca to the child-*free*. I'm still ambivalent.

I have had my own version of this argument on many occasions. I have mentioned to you before how difficult I have found it at times to talk about my sterilisation . . . not because I am in any way disturbed by discussing the issue, but because many of my feminist friends aren't comfortable when I do. (When Dora found out that I was sterilised, she was visibly sorry for me . . . obviously feels that it is a tragedy that I have been *forced* to make such a life-denying choice. I did try to explain that it was not a judgement about *children* but an assessment of a male-dominated *society* which does not cater for children. There is no way that I could have had children and still have been able to lead my present life, and I *like* my present life. But this didn't stop Dora from regretting the fact that I had missed out on so much.)

Because men devalue and deny the positive nature and power of the reproduction (and even child rearing), then of course one of the major feminist goals should be to *insist* on its value. I support that entirely. If a woman chooses to have children, then I think that society should not only rate it as one of the most important tasks that can be undertaken (after all, it *is* about the survival of the species), but I also fervently believe that it should be more than just rhetoric, and that every possible effort should be made to ensure that it has all the 'perks' of a high prestige occupation. But of course, society doesn't rate it highly and doesn't reward it – and I haven't got children!

I don't think people would mind so much at times if I went along with the idea that having decided to be child-free I now experienced some regret. But I'm not a bit sorry. I honestly don't *feel* as though I have missed out on anything . . . or indeed, that I am putting a huge amount of energy into *denying* my own sacrifice. (Deep down, I have entertained the possibility that even if children and mothers were valued, it is quite likely that I would still want to remain child-free, and abstain from being a mother . . . and I think that is what is unnerving to some women at times.) Again, it is a case of one's very existence becoming an 'affront' . . . for what does it mean if a women can say (cheerfully) that one of the better decisions she made in her life was to be child-free? It does rather undermine the notion that the peculiar and fundamental feature of women's consciousness is associated with motherhood.

I do agree with you, though, that given the history of men's treatment of women, if women are no longer necessary for the purpose of reproduction, it is quite likely that men will decide women are no longer necessary (and I have used *that* sentence in '*Feminist Theorists*'). And it does seem as though male medical technology is intent on making women no longer necessary for reproduction. Predictable of course.

If you have any brilliant solutions, please don't keep them to yourself. For my money, I will go for the explanation that male dominance began when men discovered that women did not reproduce themselves but that men played a (small) part in the process. Since that time the history of the human race has been the history of male attempts to establish that their *small* contribution is the *superior* contribution. They have really tried to do a reversal. Remember some of those beliefs that abounded in ancient Greece and Rome (and into the middle ages . . . if not today)? That the source of life was the male sperm and that women were merely the incubators, that they were but the nourishers of male-giving life; that males were the active human substance and females the passive human substance? Quite a lot of these theories have been given weight by Christianity which has the biggest reversal of all where a supposedly male god gave birth to the human species '. . . No doubt if men keep developing along the lines they have shown in the past then we can expect that in the future they will come to resemble the god they have created in their own image, and will be able to give birth to their own kind'. (Newspaper headings: 'Technology Terminates Women!) Women will have been but a stage in male evolution and Darwin will be vindicated. How's that for a 'sci-fi' version of the not-too-distant future?

Coming back to the present though, I do think that you have a point when you say that the best contraceptive is women's sexual appetite . . . and does *that* raise a lot of questions! After all, isn't this the permissive era when women have been liberated and when to many, liberation can be equated with the quest for the orgasm and the right to sex as entertainment? But I am always puzzled (like hell) about the origins of these ideas. I know that men make up the values and to me this one looks as though it very definitely emanates from men (and is in men's interests), because for the life of me I can't find many women my age (or even younger) who are prepared to state that they *like* heterosexual sex, (and of the few who do state that it is their reason for living, I have the distinct impression that they are protesting too much).

It's the same situation that I have encountered again and again in doing feminist research, where there is a deeply entrenched belief that the world works in a certain way and yet, when I *speak* to women they can individually acknowledge that the world does *not* work in the way it has been decreed. All those women who said women were the talkative sex but they – personally – didn't get much opportunity to talk; all those women who said that of course women now had access to the same education as boys but that they – personally – hadn't received the same education as their fathers or brothers. And now all these women who say that a satisfactory sex life is necessary for fulfilment but that they – personally – don't have one, or don't want one. What do you think is going on?

Undoubtedly, there has been a transformation over this century in the meaning of sexuality but as you know, I am *not* one to assume that there is progress and I *am* one who is consistently looking for the way in which men gain from new mores and meanings. And I don't think there is any doubt that men have gained greatly from the changes in sexuality in that more women are now more readily available to them than ever before, particularly with the advent of the pill. Even young women today are deprived of the excuse that you and I could engage in our youth . . . we couldn't indulge because we might get pregnant. That doesn't work any more because there is no need to get pregnant; if a woman says 'no' it can be a fair indication that she doesn't want sex (with some men, anyway) and rather than be seen as rejecting heterosexual sex, she is more often than not seen as rejecting the *man* and is accordingly condemned. So . . . women are coerced into sexual intercourse. It is much more sophisticated than brute force. (I think we should start talking about being 'sexually autonomous' – it's a more attractive label than 'celibacy', don't you agree?)

This isn't a new argument you know; it is the same one Aphra Behn used in 1670 . . . another 'permissive' age. Sometimes I don't know whether to be delighted to find that women have said all these things before, or depressed because we have to keep saying them again and again.

If I am doing a bit of heavy on you I do apologise, but with Pippa and Renate both still in the States (and Lizzie working like crazy on her PhD) I don't have my usual outlets for sounding-forth. Maybe I will have a lighter touch when Pippa gets back soon.

I do share some of your apprehensions about your male offspring and think that boarding school is definitely the answer . . . but is there a state boarding school? We can't keep up our position on state schools while the children go to private ones . . . or, I suppose we can. It seems to be the 'in' thing to do in many 'left' and 'progressive' circles.

I always enjoy hearing about the boys and have written to them both this week . . . but I must say with all honesty that not once have I ever thought it would be nice to have some of my own. Being an aunt is about the maximum I can take I think . . . a few weeks of the year (and then only for a few hours of the day), and the occasional letter. When they are a little older, I shall make them the generous offer of being available as a source of all wisdom . . . what more could they . . . or I . . . want?

Feel free this morning to sit down and talk to you without worrying about all the other things I ought to be doing. I have finished my Women and Technology essay – a review of the literature on women and science, which I called 'Should we change women or can we change science?'. You can imagine the issues that were raised. I'm wondering what the reaction will be because the assignment I did – a feminist perspective on technological change – was assessed as being too feminist! I really must try hard *not* to answer questions and to make my arguments more obscure if I want to qualify as a proper academic. Obviously, if people can understand what you are saying and the arguments are simple and sound, then it is not complex enough to be important or intellectual. What a sham education has turned out to be.

I went on Sunday to the inaugural public meeting of the Women's Political Coalition. It was quite different from the Canadian Feminist Party, although they both have the same fundamental rationale of getting more women into 'the house'. There were lots of young women there (i.e. younger than I am) and I was quite surprised to find that I was viewed as one of the wise, old women. I still think of myself as having so much to learn that I am shocked to find that I am seen as part of the older generation. Besides, I have a secret belief that if I continue to wear jeans and t-shirts, I'll stay perpetually young. Obviously I have kept this belief too much of a secret – no-one else seems to be aware of my youthfulness!

I did feel myself being attracted to the idea of politics again (I thought I had outgrown that in Canada). The idea of being in a position where it seems (erroneously) you can *do* something rather than just theorize about what should be done still pulls at me. But I am not prepared at this moment to become a 'public' figure in a male system. Too compromising and soul destroying. And I don't want to be an honorary male – having to play men's games while trying to maintain an allegiance to women . . .

Dost thou thinks't that the lady doth protest too much?

Having Jill here from Canada has resulted in my making an effort to *go out* and participate in the world. I don't like it much. We had lunch yesterday with a woman friend of a woman friend who was interested in Canada and who wanted to talk more to Jill: and *there were men there*. One was 'a proper arsehole' (Canadian terminology) who has just 'travelled to forty-nine countries the world over' and who took me seriously when I asked why he felt it important to keep count of the countries he had visited. The other one did not speak for the entire afternoon and I could not decide whether he was *listening* to what we were saying so that he could use it against us later, or whether he had *switched off* because we were talking 'women's talk'. I did not entertain the possibility that he may have had other motives. I have yet to meet the Australian male who is genuinely interested in learning from women.

By the way, I was delighted to learn from your letter that V-Day had been and gone without any signs of rationing. It just goes to show that progress is being made. Perhaps next time around, Maggie will be able to organize a V-Day without a war as well. Sounds reasonable to me.

Your index for '*Women of Ideas*' sounds marvellous and without having ever named it as a particular activity, it is sort of what I tried to do with the index for '*Intruders*'. Now that I see it as a conscious effort to reconceptualize 'knowledge', I wish I could re-do the index – a far less formidable task for a book of 150 pages than for one with 600 pages. I also know how you feel about your back. Can you get a chair with more support . . . do an exercise programme to strengthen your neck muscles . . . hang from the rafters for an hour a day – or just spend a little less time at your desk? It would be a shame if our years in our feminist retirement retreat were spent with me pushing you around in a wheel-chair while I tended the tomato plants *and* put the garbage out. Seriously, do be careful and listen to your body when it start to tell you *enough*. You've still got a few years left, you know, to read and write all those books. A late starter you may be, but in the long run, I don't think it will matter much if you only produce four books a year instead of six. Even twenty years at four a year is eighty books – and you'd still only be as old as Rebecca's daughter . . . the mind boggles . . .

So, in the world of journalism, you're not humorous enough and I'm not sufficiently substantial. It does put us in good company with Aphra Behn, Mary Wollstonecraft, etc. And yes, I have quite recovered from my disappointment and can view the whole episode as amusing and totally predictable. Women have to be 'wrong' if men are to be 'right'. It's like having to know about cold before you can understand hot. Adrienne Rich says that objectively (with all its positive connotations) is simply the name men have given to their own (emotional) view of the world so that they can label women's alternative view as subjective – with all its connotations of emotionalism and irrationality. The power to name. It's a power that men have taken and used to name everything about themselves as postive, strong and worthwhile and everything about women as inferior and of less value. Matilda Joslyn Gage knew this last century when she pointed out that in spite of all the evidence that it was men who, in war, rape and even at their football matches, exhibited 'ungovernable frenzy', it was still women who were named as the emotional ones . . . or am I being too emotional about all this?

I have resisted becoming emotional this week in relation to the children and have had to call on a snippet of information that I picked up somewhere – years ago. I read in a biography of a great man (at the time when I still read books about men) that children who were raised according to a policy of 'benign neglect' were more likely to achieve in a big wide world than those who were cosseted and catered for. A handy piece of information – especially when I am aware that Jay and Aaron have had to do quite a bit of fending for themselves while I have been completing assignments. I think Jay probably qualifies technically as a 'latchkey' child but I also think it does him no harm. He seems quite happy to come home and prepare a snack (he doesn't have to check with me, and can put layers of peanut butter and jam onto fresh bread) and several afternoons he has spent hours drawing innumerable versions of the harbour bridge. (I've enclosed one for you.) The only problem is deciding what to do with 20 or so drawings of a bridge. I tend to throw them out as soon as he is not looking but we have had several scenes where they have had to be retrieved from the garbage. Aaron, less concerned about the material world, is perfectly happy to stay at his pre-school until 5.00 p.m. In fact, he would rather be there after most of the other children have gone so that he can be the centre of attention . . . perhaps I have one artist and one actor in the making. Under those circumstances, the least I can do is make sure that I am often late home so that Jay can practise his drawing without interruption and so that Aaron can practise performing for a sympathetic audience. What a good mother I am!

I have had a lot of laughs at Jill's reaction to Australian culture . . . It's a delight to see the world through a different pair of eyes. She was quite puzzled by a reference to the 'Australian salute' (swatting at flies around the face) and chuckled at us having 'brekky'. I, on the other hand, was puzzled by her attributing her inability to eat left-overs (cold lamb) to her 'lower class' upbringing and instead opting to eat fish and chips! A mismatch in my value system and good for both of us to have to come to terms with different ways of looking at things. I think that you are right in saying that the only thing that is certain is that if we are both alive, we shall continue to write to each other. That's pretty good security.

I picked up on your idea of sterilization and whether or not it represents a denial of women's power. Seems to me that I have had a great deal more power to plan things and get them done since I've not had to deal with a fear of pregnancy or the inconvenience of contraception. That, however, is quite different from power *over* others and perhaps I need to spend a little time considering just what 'power' is. Meanwhile, I am struck at the possible connections between sterilization and menopause. If so many of the problems associated with menopause stem from women coming to terms with the end of their 'functional' existence, does that mean that women who have chosen to be sterilized should

(a) experience an identity crisis and post-sterilization depression
(b) have no problems at all at physical menopause
(c) contact the nearest feminist publisher and make up their own story about menopause.

I think a light and mocking exposé of the myths of menopause should be written but I suppose it might not be politically correct. What do you think? It has also just occurred to me that my political concerns with menopause may stem directly from my personal concern with advancing age. I will be thirty-six next month (and still in jeans!). The personal is political in more ways than one.

Aaron sends thanks for his letter – Jay is writing his own reply. I have decided to cease threatening them with the possibility of boarding school on the grounds that by the time they reach high school, they will be the only children left in the state school system and will have lots of individual attention. According to the Australian press, parents (including and even featuring the left-wing trendies) are withdrawing their children 'in droves' from the state system and wives are taking on second jobs to pay for the 'discipline' and 'commitment' (to what, one might ask) that private school education allegedly offers.

Could it be that private schools are actually offering a return to 'the good old days' (very appealing to those now in the establishment who see their education as the source of their success), while the state schools are being freed to explore new ways and means of dealing with a changing society (not so appealing to those who have reached the top and don't want any change)? Either way, I hope the debate continues. I saw Ruth during the week and she says that the issue provides a major talking point at country dinners amongst the New England squattocracy. It would be a shame for them to have to waste time dealing with petty educational issues like the preferential treatment for boys that is offered quite openly in *both* school systems. I wouder how many parents still send their sons to private schools and their daughters to the local high school. Maybe that's the explanation for females generally doing better in their Higher School Certificate. Ha! You know that they weighted male results here to allow more boys to enter into Teachers' Colleges. I think I shall write to Ruth with that one and see what she can do with it. There is, of course, the chance that she will write back and tell *me* what to do with it – in good Australian vernacular . . .

You *are* a proper rotter. I woke up early this morning but as it was Saturday decided that even I should have the occasional self-indulgent doze in bed, and so I just stayed there in semi-dreamland for a while, only to be informed by an irate Ted that I was snoring so loudly that the neighbours would be worrying that the war was *not* over and that bombs were dropping on London.

Now I do not like to know that I snore, partly because there is nothing that I can do about it. I don't want to snore, I don't snore deliberately, and I find the whole idea of snoring – and of being a snorer – quite repulsive. So except for the times when I actually wake myself up with my snoring I prefer to remain oblivious to this aesthetically unpleasing habit over which I have no control and which I cannot, therefore, change.

After this distressing start to my day, I had to put considerable energy into re-establishing my feeling of well-being and had just begun to meet with sufficient success to cope with the post, when I opened a letter from you. It contained that press clipping which boldly declared that DRINK CAN KILL YOU RESEARCHERS WARN SNORERS. I was back to wishing that the day had not begun!

Why do you do this to me? That first paragraph sent chills of terror up my spine . . . 'If you drink and snore, chances are that your brain is shrinking'. How can I cope with such an onslaught?

Over the last few years I have learnt to rationalise my drinking and even to take some consolation, in the proven loss of brain cells which drinking produces, with the idea that if I hadn't drunk so much in my youth, I would have been a wizard now instead of merely competent. But you have ruined my resigned state of mind.

To drink too much, to smoke and to snore, is more than can be tolerated. You have caused me to resort to self-hatred (and I still haven't lost the 8 lbs). The only ray of sunshine on the horizon was the realization that some people are worse off than I am. Think of the researchers behind this latest discovery.

They say that they have measured the size of the brain of people who have died of drunken snoring, and it is demonstrable that those who drink and snore do have shrunken brains. There can't be many worse ways of earning your living than measuring drinking, snoring, shrunken brains.

As no mention is made in the article of overweight or sore backs from bending over a desk, I am obviously *not* a representative drinker/snorer with a shrunken brain. I shall take refuge in this uncontrolled variable.

It really is a giggly article, isn't it? When you can prove anything with research, why do people persist in proving things like this? I am much more sympathetic to the Australian researcher who proved that smoking was good for you. At least I felt better after reading his reports. I often use him as a case study when talking about research and how you can make it do (almost) anything you want it to. When all the information that we had about smoking came from questions which were directed at establishing how harmful it was, you couldn't possibly have got *his* results. I think it's superb that he asked questions about the good things that came from smoking and found that smokers had more friends, were less irritable, more sociable, and less prone to stress and tension. (I wonder why the tobacco companies haven't adopted that line? It almost makes you lose faith in the evils of capitalism when such a good opportunity is missed.)

Mrs Thatcher, however, doesn't appear to be missing many opportunities when it comes to making sure that unemployment is not a big public issue. For weeks now, I have admired her cunning in keeping the dismal picture off the front page (and keeping the focus off the government's cynical policy of creating two classes of people, the 'haves' and 'have-nots') and I did think there would be every chance she would be called to account once the war had ceased to be the main news story of the day. But no, no sooner does the war end than Mrs Thatcher obviously organises the Princess Diana to give birth and once more the government gets a reprieve.

Now you would think that would just about exhaust her luck. I fully expected that this week, once the hubbub of the royal birth had subsided, we might get an examination of unemployment and the reasons for it. But what do I find spread all across my newspaper this morning? The announcement that the Queen's bodyguard is a homosexual, and that while England may be able to win conventional wars, its security measures do not meet conventional criteria. With announcements like that there is no room for unemployment statistics to follow.

Perhaps the protest that I await will not come. I find that difficult to believe. It might not take the form I want it to (and be a widespread recognition that economics is nothing other than a superstitious belief system which does little or nothing to explain the world) but I can't accept that almost five million people will docilely retreat to a subsistence level existence because a few gurus (who cannot agree among themselves on the omens or the signs) have delivered their prophecies and said that such immoral inequality is neccessary for survival. Even the medieval mystics . . . and Newton for that matter . . . had a better line in wild explanations.

There is simply no way that I can take economics or economists seriously. As far as I am concerned, we have another case of a male dominated institution where a group of men have sat around and with great solemnity decided that what they do is work, but what women do is not work. Having made that crucial and imaginative distinction which defies all evidence – and serves as another illustration of the potential of men to believe anything they choose as long as it is in their own interest – they have then proceeded to declare that because they are the self-defined workers, they are entitled to cash rewards.

Of course there have been a few complications along the way and they have often been required to massage the evidence. There have been occasions when men have engaged in the non-work that women customarily perform . . . like cooking, or cleaning, or even sewing. But that has been readily resolved by the rule that when men do it, it goes by a different name and can therefore count as work and be paid. Thus we have chefs, contract cleaners, and tailors. You know what Margaret Mead said, the world over men may weave, or hunt humming birds or make magic, and whenever men engage in these activites the whole society grants them significance and deems them worthy of reward . . . but whenever women do them, the whole society sees it as menial, if not invisible.

And even the United Nations is backing up Mead these days. I note that the statistics for third world countries suggest that in many (if not most of them), the majority of the agricultural labour is performed by women and when performed by women it does not count as part of the GNP (another neat male invention). So we have all these crops growing in third world countries and they are mainly produced by non-work. Of course you can't take economics seriously. When the same non-work is performed by men it counts as work.

All these men in our own society running round saying that we have evolved into a cash economy . . . what sort of a mockery does that make of all the dependent women? Such women are in no different a position from their serf forbears . . . exchanging services in support for board and lodging . . . not much cash there.

Sometimes I lose my sense of humour and just get plain mad. Men own 99 per cent of the world's resources and the gap between women's and men's earnings grows greater every year, and they sit there and prove with their theories that we have equal pay now, and that there is no sex discrimination in the work force. You couldn't possibly trust anyone who was able to reach those conclusions from the present statistics.

For women, economics is much the same as it has been for centuries . . . it is sexual economics. With only 1 per cent of the world's resources, it simply isn't enough to go round and if women (and more often than not their children) are to survive, then women have to get access to those resources. And how is it done? Women are obliged to trade themselves in order to survive. But that doesn't come into conventional economics.

It is a common understanding among women that men who are happy, pay more . . . and so we see women the world over trying to create the goodwill of men. Even Virginia Woolf knew she was talking about economics and survival when she said that for centuries women have been acting as looking glasses for men, reflecting them at twice their normal size: (good lordess, men can't believe it's *natural* for women to flatter them, or that women like doing it, can they? I suppose all things are possible, particularly when you see what other absurdities men seem prepared to believe). If I was going to devise a theory of economics, a theory for explaining the distribution of resources, one of the first things I would include at the moment would be the enormous amount of energy women have to put into making men feel good . . . so men can pay the bills.

It doesn't matter much whether it is your employer or your husband, basically the man whose ego is managed, delivers more of the goods and when women need the goods, they manage the egos . . . beautifully at times.

But there is no category in the GNP for the number of woman-hours expended in ego massage . . . let alone all of those hours (and days and years) that are spent on the non-work of housework and child care.

If women were paid for their non-work of course then the male response would be to say that there was no way society could afford women . . . and that is a real misogynist trap, isn't it? But as it stands at the moment, I think that economics is a 'science' of the absurd, that there is not one shred of evidence that it explains what it states it sets out to do, and instead of being astonished that the predictions of the economists are always wrong, I am astonished that people can think it sensible to *pay* them for the work they do. As you know, I'm quite keen on the idea that people should be allowed to pursue knowledge for its own sake, for the kick it gives them, and I have no objections to people using their time to study anything from prescriptive grammar to the 'secret of life' (which some call the structure of DNA and I call alchemy). But I don't think society should be obliged to reward them for their esoteric studies or be forced to listen to their findings, and I think economists should find their own means of support. Perhaps they could try and cultivate the good will of the occasional wealthy woman . . . no doubt it would make a difference to their consciousness if they did, and they could well start to develop theories along the lines that those who control the purse strings are also entitled to flattery.

That Keynes developed his economic theories as a hobby . . . and for a bit of a game, has always appealed to me. How could he have known people would take him seriously and try to make a whole society conform to his rules? You don't have to be brilliant to work out that a society based on everyone buying at the cheapest and selling at the dearest is bound to have limited success . . . (I can remember as a kid thinking that sooner or later that would have to collapse), but I think you have to be a positive dunce to go along with some of the present so-called solutions.

Both capitalism and socialism as they have been explained and ordered by man have one thing (at least) in common. They are both systems that have to expand . . . they are both based on the ideology of industrialisation which demands that every year more and more is produced . . . and consumed. And it isn't just that I think this whole approach is nonsensical . . . I also object to such an ideology on ethical grounds. Think what value system lies behind such practices! We are deliberately creating human beings who, from an early age, have instilled in them the necessity of needing *more* next year; no great attention is given to more of *what*; it is quantity not quality which is the crucial factor. I think it is a philosophy of *greed*. I think it is directly associated with the morality of mastery . . . and I think that as a philosophy it is offensive.

But I find the present unemployment even more offensive. I think it is immoral and indefensible for one group of gurus who currently enjoy some power to inflict so much misery and demoralisation on so many 'other' human beings on the basis of the gurus' own future profit.

It's possible to prove anything within a given system, including economics, although the economists don't seem to have been too familiar with that premise either . . . their record in the 'proof department' leaves a lot to be desired. It would be just as possible to prove that at the moment the best thing for society would be full employment . . . but of course there would be a redistribution of some of the existing resources if that line were adopted. Looking at the profile of those who enjoy power, it isn't likely that such a prophecy will descend from the gods in the near future.

Sometimes I think I will just give in to despair. I was listening to one of the tapes I made with Constance Rover last night (for *'There's Always Been a Women's Movement'*) and in it she said that it could be that when historians come to look back on the seventies, they could well decide that it was one of the worst times for women, because they took on so much extra work without shedding any of the traditional work. She was referring to the fact that the phenomenon of the double-shift which working class women have always had to endure, spread in the seventies to middle class women as well. For the first time really, middle class women were asked to take on some of the responsibility of being the breadwinner . . . but without the status or privilege, without benefit of equal pay . . . and without being relieved of much of the work they had traditionally done.

It hasn't been phrased in that way of course. It has taken the form of men stating that the desirable women these days are ones who have interesting little careers – careers which are sufficient to take some of the pressure off men but not sufficient to be threatening. The modern man evidently isn't interested in 'just a housewife' any more but wants a partner (this is someone who will be a partner in earning the money) and so we have the rise of superwoman, who still has children and family to look after, as well as the additional task of money earning.

And all the time the gap between women's and men's earnings grows greater. Matilda Joslyn Gage was right . . . the harder women work, the richer men get. Hilda Scott says that it is getting to be such a huge discrepancy that by the year 2000, poverty will be exclusively a female problem.*

I have thought about this a lot. Ninety-nine percent of the world's resources in male hands and they are accumulating more every year. For centuries women have been insisting that there can be no independence for women *without* economic independence and it seems to me that men have been listening, and have been convinced of the argument . . . with the result that they have made sure that *fewer*, not *more* resources, fall into women's hands. Another example of male resistance.

So what are we going to do about it? There doesn't seem to be much point in lecturing, or lamenting . . . and I am beyond laughing . . . It's a systematic programme that we need to redistribute the world's resources.

And on that basis, I am making a serious proposal. That all good feminists should take it as a personal goal . . . in the interest of women's cause . . . *to separate a man from his money.* Any man. All men. It should be seen as something that every woman could do to help her sisters.

If all women were so committed, we could well have a 'quiet' revolution, a rechannelling of resources (I believe this happens sometimes among men on the stock exchange), and by the year 2000 we could have a reversal. Men could wake up one morning and find women hold the purse strings . . . and it would all be over. Patriarchy pricked and powerless. What joy . . . what celebration then!

In the interim I suppose we have to deal with the power that prevails. It is fine to have one foot in the future and to constantly envisage what the world *could* be – but it seems to me that it's necessary to keep the other foot firmly planted in the present, and patriarchy. We do have to live, work and *eat* in the here and now as I keep telling some of my (younger) women friends who are doing their PhDs. They are having problems and partly because they insist on behaving as if it is an ideal world and not the power-based one we do inhabit.

---

* See Hilda Scott, '*The Feminization of Poverty*, Pandora Press.

I don't seem to be able to convince them that PhD students have *less* power than other students. In their terms, because they have moved up the hierarchy and are in the 'advanced' stages of education, they believe that they have little to prove and that their supervisors are more like consultants, than judges. I don't see it that way, and I am sure I am not just plain cynical. There is safety and security in numbers and a class of students has more bargaining power as far as I am concerned than a single PhD student who is usually involved in a one-to-one relationship with a supervisor – and the supervisor has supreme power!

I've been trying to tell some of my friends that supervisors have their own reputations to guard, their own body of work to protect, and they can be very closed-minded people, the last to want to entertain new ideas and methods which challenge the validity of their life's work. But my words seem to fall on deaf ears. A couple of the women are so sure that the point of a PhD exercise is intellectual excellence (whatever that may mean) and that the more original, illuminating and substantive their work may be – the more assured they are of passing. They all set out with meaningful human questions for which they passionately require answers, on the assumption that when they find out we will be that much closer to solving the world's problems. Is there no hope? Don't they realise how many people (including their supervisors) have an investment in the 'problems' and want to keep it that way?

I have explained that their approach is *no way* to do a PhD, that what is going on is a test which is not of course made public, or open to scrutiny. Their supervisors are members of a very exclusive club with secret rules for membership, and to get a PhD you have to work out those rules and put forward a convincing case that you are a perfectly proper candidate for the club. As the substance of some of my friends' PhDs is the necessity of blowing up such exclusive clubs (one is on Woman's Studies and its absence of hierarchies, as a superior form of education), I don't like their chances of qualifying for membership. When you combine their content with their conviction that their PhD will be a useful – and much used –

welcome addition to the reservoirs of the world's knowledge, I just throw up my hands in horror – and give in!

I wish '*Women of Ideas – and What Men Have Done to Them*' – was available. Then I could let them see that for centuries women have been putting forward 'solutions' to some of the most persistent and pernicious problems – and men have been discarding and dismissing those solutions so that it is as if they were never put forward. But I don't seem to be able to explain that in a five minute 'chat' . . . although I have got them to look at the parallels with conversation. 'Do your supervisors *listen* to your ideas when you talk to them?' I asked, 'or is it as if you hadn't spoken, and your ideas are just ignored?' And of course they know they are not heard – but they still retain the belief that all will be different when bound between the blue hard cover of their PhD dissertations.

I suppose what really unsettles them is the fact that a few of them have feminist supervisors and they expect feminist treatment. But that is just so unrealistic. Often feminist academics are even more suspect, and the hierarchy keeps an even closer watch over the members they admit to the club, with the result that the feminist supervisor has to show an even greater commitment than the non-feminist to the rules of so-called rigour and scholarship. Women just don't have power that isn't accountable to men, and so they aren't free to choose their forms of behaviour, but are forced to act in ways that men will approve – and that goes for Mrs Thatcher as well as feminist academics. I don't know, I thought the basic lesson in feminism was to understand that in a patriarchal society women's options are circumscribed, and that's why feminism is necessary. But here they are as PhD students acting as if feminist supervisors are free, autonomous beings who are wilfully (evidently because of some hormone imbalance or flaw in their feminine character) obstructing their students.

Even my description of Ted's students was spectacularly unsuccessful when it came to getting them to reassess what they were doing. I told them about some of Ted's boys who work out what the current issues are in the market place, who carefully select one which is manageable in research terms (about eighteen months to two years), who then proceed to get funding – usually from a company which is interested in the answer – and then uneventfully pass through the required stages. With the greatest disinterest (which is called 'objectivity' and is applauded) they prove their suitability as members for the exclusive club; they get a job and the 'perks', and the system continues without challenge or interruption.

Meanwhile, there are these serious and committed women asking their massively meaningful questions which are not at all manageable. They are so 'emotionally involved' in the question, the answer – and even the methodology – that from the outset they are accused of excessive subjectivity and an absence of scholarly criteria. They are obliged to take five – not two years – to gather their data (and then they have to spend a year sorting it, and agonising over what to leave out); they construct problem after problem for themselves, and they do it all without funding. Because they genuinely want answers, they are dismissed for their personal involvement and because their answers are rarely flattering to their supervisors – or the establishment – there is, *predictably*, considerable resistance to the acceptance of their 'sub-standard' theses which they have taken so long to submit (and been so troublesome and demanding on the way) – *and there is no good job at the end*. Few want to hear the feminist answers!

It really comes down to why they want their PhDs . . . If they want to demonstrate their ability to jump through male hoops (and to show that it is not particularly difficult), to get the bit of paper which advertises membership of the club, then it's a fairly simple procedure – as Ted's students demonstrate. But if they want to do some *meaningful*, research and write it up, they should write a book – for people who might want to understand. There's no evidence that supervisors and examiners want to know or understand. They want to protect and guard the existing body of knowledge which validates their existence.

I know if I were a male I'd just be horrified with the work some of the women are doing. I'd be outraged . . . and I certainly wouldn't give them PhDs.

Oh well, I guess this is how the world works. You can tell Jay that my offer still stands . . . he doesn't have to believe anything he's taught in school, he can continue to keep his chart on 'The biggest lie I was told today by my superiors' and if ever he wants the paper qualifications, it will only take a couple of days to teach him the rules. He need not worry about 'passing' until he decides where he wants to go.

And the Harbour Bridge arrived – many thanks. Have sent the Albert Bridge in return.

I recognise that my letters have been longer lately – put it down to the absence of my conversational partners. Pippa will be home next week and can relieve you of responding to my wrath.

⚥ Coogee, July 1982

Have finally surfaced to-day after a morning in bed (dragged myself up to take the children to school) because I over-ate, over-drank and generally over-indulged myself last night in celebration of my 36th year. I went to lunch with Lorraine and then out to supper last night with Graeme, Penny and Sue, and I have absolutely no desire to eat, drink or inhale on a cigarette again until my 37th birthday – and even then, I'll think twice. How awful to still be unable to make connections between one's behaviour and its results – before the event rather than afterwards.

You will please bear with me if the typing errors are even worse than usual to-day for I have, on stopping for a moment, realized that I am suffering from a form of the DTs. Now this may be due to the cold – am putting the heater on, just in case, but it may also be due to my wanton behaviour! Not only did I drink and smoke last night, I was loud, argumentative, rude, etc. and took up a great deal of space. Does this all sound familiar? Should I feel ashamed or feel that I have 'vindicated' my female training at least one night in the year?

To more pleasant issues!

I have received a written offer from the New South Wales Institute of Technology to enrol in law. Apparently the Dean did recommend that I be accepted as a student and enrolment is on 27th July and lectures commence shortly afterwards.

There will be a fair amount of juggling in the family in order to accommodate additional lectures but I guess we'll survive. Keep telling myself that the less I do for the children, the more they will do for themselves and the better off we'll all be. I still have trouble coming to terms with the notion that there is some value in keeping children dependent and in need of you. Seems pretty silly to me. I wonder if I will ever look back and say 'I wish I'd spent more time with them when they were little'. Don't think so.

I did take last Saturday 'off' from writing and took the kids into town to the Museum and then to the movies. There is no doubt that the movies and the constant chatter are far more demanding than writing. We saw '*The Man from Snowy River*' – which the kids loved – or I should say, Jay loved. Aaron was far more interested in popcorn, drinks and how much longer we would be. There were, of course, no women in the movie – except as foils for men and as the 'other' half in demonstrations of *man's* infinite capacity for love, courage and physical prowess. The movie had every possible ingredient of the typical boys' adventure story. A 'baddie' or two, a love affair (youthful, naturally), hard drinking, hard riding, a 'black sheep' who turns out to be white and a real boy's passage to manhood. What more could any *boy* want? Jay was totally 'sucked-in' by it all and cried tears of passion, pain and pleasure. He was 'proud' he said, of the man from Snowy River and hopes he can grow up to be as true and as brave, Aaron, less articulate, has simply decided that he will change his name to 'Jim' (the hero of the story) and I suppose that is his way of saying that he too was impressed.

'Jim' has subsequently refused to answer any questions or to respond to any requests unless he is addressed as 'Jim'. Very cunning. He still hears what he wants to hear but manages to avoid any issue that might interfere with his time or space. I'm reluctant to think that his is a demonstration at *four years of age* of a male power-play but can see that it could develop into one – if I humour him and think how cute he is. You know that awful tendency that men have to 'miss' what you say the first times and then later, demand that you repeat it – when they *want* to listen (and when you are talking to somebody else about something entirely different – which excludes them). That's a power play which makes women accommodate men on men's terms. It means not only that you have to massage their egos by proving that the world will stop, go back and pick them up – if they wish it – but also that you have to deny your own importance in favour of men. It also works remarkably well to make sure that you have less time available for *self*. If you have to be available to repeat yourself – to say everything twice – it cuts back on your time to think of and make new connections. I can see how it also sets us up very well for men to turn around and tell us we're the 'talkative' sex.

Think I'll have to start ignoring 'Jim'!

Had a good chuckle at your reaction to the snoring article. I don't feel in the least repentant nor am I at all intimidated by your objections to my sending it to you. Do you remember what you sent me after I had my second *male* child? The story of a women who dressed her male children as girls in an attempt to order the world so that she'd feel positive about her life and her children rather than negative.* I still haven't worked out whether you were trying to stir me out of intellectual lethargy or whether you were providing me with evidence that I was not the only woman in the world disappointed by having only male offspring.

Rather a turn-around isn't it?

We have always been led to believe that sons were the joy of their mother's existence, but talking to my women friends, I'm sure that Verity Bargate and I did not have some weird, one-off existence. To value male children over female seems to me to be a reflection of society's (read men's) power to impose particular economic and personal values on women – and to have some women accept them.

The children have a friend who comes to visit sometimes – his mother brings him and from her comments I am aware of a huge gap between the way she sees her son and the way I see

---

* 'No Mamma No' written by Verity Bargate who died of cancer in 1982.

him. She refers to him – usually in front of him – in terms that elevate him into some sort of mature, reliable husband-substitute. He 'looks after her'. Yet, from what I can see he is an ordinary, rather sneaky little boy to whom she has to speak three times before he listens and who, even then, disregards what she has to say. How can the difference in our views be explained? I know that people are very selective in what they see and in the way they explain what they 'see', but surely there has to be some evidence on which to base your assessments. Perhaps it comes down to the fact that in comparison to her husband, the minute offspring does seem to show her more care and concern. But I still can't see how or why a mature adult woman could encourage a small boy who can't even read yet, to believe that she needed him to help her solve her problems. Beats me – and bodes ill, methinks, for that young man's view of his own importance (and his mother's incompetence!) in a few years time.

What's that old saying? (An old *wives* tale?) – 'That daughters are daughters all your life but sons are sons till they take a wife.' That's been interpreted as one of the reasons women shouldn't get along with sons-in-law (who take their daughters away) or with daughters-in-law (who take their sons away). The old mother-in-law myths. But it could also reflect women's joy in having daughters and in the possibility of a lifetime of shared experiences. I'm staying with the latter interpretation. Mum knew when I had Aaron that I was initially disappointed. She maintained that it wasn't so bad because at least I had a mother and a sister to share my experience with – some women have neither. Typically mum! Reconstruct events to make them positive rather than negative. I ended up feeling grateful rather than resentful. Still today, I am delighted when Jay and Aaron paint their faces and dress up but I think that I'd be horrified if either of them was female. If I saw them painting their faces or putting on make-up for any reason other than fun. I think I'd go berserk. Some of the worst experiences that my feminist friends talk about come from watching their daughters go through that stage of moulding themselves to be attractive to men. As if their lives depended on male approval. The awful irony is that while society stays the way it is, male approval does appear to be the easiest and most obvious path to 'success'. Imagine watching a daughter go through all that and then watching while she finds out that it doesn't work in the long run.

Great to have sons, I say!

We too have had news this week of trauma in the Royal family. Australians cannot only manufacture their own scandals to keep genuinely 'moral' issues off the front page, they can use the Royal Family too! We have been regaled at various times with the horrors of Margaret's life, the imminent breakdown of the marriage of Anne and Mark, and now we have men in the Queen's bedroom and homosexuals on the security staff.

I don't think anyone really regards the Royal revelations as anything other than titillation and fairy stories. However, they do serve, as you say, to preclude any serious discussion or evaluation of unemployment or the failure of the 'system' to satisfy the needs and interests of more than the few at the top. I suppose to your economic 'gurus' satisfying the needs of those at the top is a sign of success rather than failure. All of 'us' on the lower rungs of the ladder can really only hang on in the hope that we don't fall off altogether.

Certainly there are no signs of revolt here – in spite of rising unemployment and the beginnings of a 'revolution' in terms of job-sharing and part-time work.

But of course, that is not seen as a revolution. Revolutions, men tell us, consist of *man*ning the barricades, of physical violence and disorder and as far as I'm concerned, of the ultimate replacement of one set of tyrants with another. 'Ejaculatory politics' as Lizzie* calls it. The visible, short, sharp burst and then it's all over and nothing has really changed. The mind boggles at their idea of that other male characteristic – premature ejaculation – also having political and economic implications. I think I could establish a

---

* Scarlet Friedman and Elizabeth Sarah (eds), '*On the Problem of Men*', The Women's Press, London 1982.

reasonable argument that male sexuality (as men have developed it) provides the model for their emotional and intellectual limitations – or perhaps it's vice-versa!

Meanwhile, we can afford a quiet snigger . . . (who says feminists are humourless?) The real revolution that is taking place is in the minds of women like us who simply do not believe men anymore.

In relation to your observations about sexual economics, there was an article in one of the Sunday papers recently about the value of women's non-work in the home. It was *not* on the front page although other information about 'economics' took up a fair amount of space. The article claimed that the non-work of the 'average' Australian housewife was worth $28,000 a year (Lisa Leghorn and Kathy Parker* suggested $35,000 a year in the US – perhaps the commitment to germ warfare is higher there!). When you think that 50 percent of Australian women are also in the paid workforce, we should all be incredibly wealthy. The explanation must lie in the system that allows men – generally and specifically – to appropriate women's work and creativity and to distribute its profits according to men's needs and interests. Marriage is fundamental to that system and has become the institutionalized and unchallenged way of arranging resources in men's favour.

Talking about marriage – I'm still at work on the manuscript and as always, I'm having trouble standing back from it far enough to comment in a relatively detached way. I did come up with some interesting thoughts about women and marriage and am trying to get them in so that they emphasise how much we take for granted our second class-citizenship . . . e.g.

Did you know . . .

1. how few situations there are when someone is actually paid to come and take goods away? There is the garbage man, the rag-and-bone man and the husband. Whether the husband is paid subtly by the wife's parents in the form of the wedding as they 'give her away' or whether there is a specific

---

* Lisa Leghorn and Kathy Parker, '*Women's Worth*', Routledge & Kegan Paul.

dowry paid, there aren't any other occasions that I can think of – offhand of course – where goods are disposed of in this way . . .

2. that marriage is probably the only career for women where previous, on-the-job-experience is of no value in applying for a new position as a wife. In fact, it seems to me that in spite of the alleged increase in pre-marital sexual promiscuity, most men still want to think that their wives qualify as new rather than used goods . . .

Tell me, how I do make that light-hearted and acceptable to a 'wide, general audience'?

Sorry to leave you with such serious thoughts but they are niggling a bit at the moment . . . besides what else are sisters for? I suppose you could say I'm having a practice-writing-run . . . trying to sort the ideas out . . .

✽ *Chelsea, July 1982*

Pippa arrived back yesterday. I was going to meet her at the airport because I thought she would probably be trying to carry two hundred books again and that she would probably break her arm. But there was a tube strike and it was too difficult to get out there. So I sent her a telegram at Heathrow telling her that there was a strike but that I still expected her to get here for breakfast. I thought she'd be here about 9.00 a.m. but it was almost 11.00 when she arrived. She got the telegram . . . and a cab (it took almost two hours in the cab) and arrived carrying two hundred books and manuscripts as I expected.

It was such a relief to see her again and to talk, particularly about everything that is going on in the States . . . even if she did have jet lag and often had to be asked the same question twice . . . and then have her answer translated before it could be understood. We were nowhere near finished talking about all the things we wanted to and it was about 1.00 so I suggested we go up the street and have something to eat . . . there being nothing to eat here as you can imagine, and nowhere to eat it anyway since the one remaining 'table' in the place got converted into a 'desk' (and became a source of philosophical discussion about what is reality).

So we went up the road to a wine bar and had some cheese and a glass of wine (talking all the time; I am sure that if we had taped ourselves it would have invalidated my research on the cooperative talk of women; I think we over-talked and interrupted each other fairly frequently), and we got back here about 3.00 p.m.

The outside wooden door was closed, which did strike me as a bit strange because no one ever does close it and I knew it had been open when I left. But I wasn't unduly perturbed. I was still talking sensibly to Pippa when I opened the wooden door and saw the glass door. Then I really did get a shock. There was a hole cut in the glass door. It was just above the lock. And it was a very neat and professional looking hole which obviously allowed you to put your hand through and open the door from the inside.

Very strange I thought. And then . . . 'Bloody robbers! Again!'

I tried to explain to Pippa that there could well be robbers inside the building but I don't think she really comprehended. After having patiently tried to explain the significance of a hole in the glass door, I skipped across to the off-licence because I know they have a direct line to the police. I asked them to ring for me and to say I thought I was being robbed.

Then I went back to Pippa who was by this time sitting on the fence and idly watching the passing traffic. I positioned myself so that I could see if anyone came out of the building (carrying a television set) and continued to try and persuade Pippa that this was serious, and that it was highly likely that there were *men* inside (the probability that it was female robbers was distinctly remote). But she didn't seem to want to be convinced and after a while I gave up. I even began to think that maybe I was panicking over nothing and that I would look pretty silly if the police arrived and it turned out to be that one of the other tenants had lost their key and had cut a hole in the door to get in. I suppose there were lots of reasons (although I can't exactly think of them at the moment), but I decided that we might as well go in. It was pretty anticlimactic sitting out there on the fence.

By this stage Pippa has entered into the spirit of the adventure and bravely bore a corkscrew in front of her. Needless to say it is a 'weapon' she is rarely without, (she had no others and I didn't even have the statutory hair pin), and so with much bravado we proceeded to go up and round the stair well, banging on every door, and calling for the robbers to come forth and show their cowardly faces.

This they obligingly did, but not before we had reached the top landing and my flat. And there they were. Two *white* men trying to break the wall down because the door wouldn't give.

I was pretty put out. It was my best school-marm voice (reserved for naughty big boys) that came bursting forth, and I loudly demanded to know what they thought they were doing. Superfluous, of course, under the circumstances, but it seemed a sensible initial question at the time. And first of all they looked so guilty (real naughty boys caught in the act) and stammered a bit, and said they were looking for someone . . . Well, I ask you?

I lost my cool. Evidently according to eye witnesses (Pippa being the primary one), my language was appalling. Both boys ran towards us after they had recovered from their shock and the front one pushed me and went to wallop me. And that was really too much. No split second while I gave myself permission to hit . . . I just lost my temper I think when I saw him coming towards me with a pretty vicious look on his face. I kicked out and I know from the state of my toes that I must have made a connection.

So much for my pacifism. And over property too. Wouldn't you think I could have been more understanding? It does raise questions about whether pacifism is an indulgence allowed to those who aren't threatened. Given my response to two 25-year-old boys trying to break down a wall I am now reasonably sure that I would have killed Hitler. So much for my non-violence.

I was sufficiently threatening (and violent) to make the second boy think better of trying to pass me. He leapt over the banisters and it was quite a drop. They both went off limping (one kicked, no doubt, and one injured from the fall), but by this time I was a heap on the floor, having fallen on top of Pippa who not only found herself digging her corkscrew into me, but was dazedly wondering how the movie in the plane had got off the screen.

The two boys careered down the stairs as fast as their limps would let them and I shouted (with some venom) that the 'police were at the bottom of the stairs waiting for them. They did stop, but just for a second. They looked up at me and then went off down the stairs again, and I suspect that they decided to take their chances with the police rather than me. I must admit that my language was still quite rich and resonant and that I probably did look fairly ferocious, and that with Pippa behind me, looking quite 'out of this world' and still brandishing her corkscrew, it was no doubt a sensible decision on their part to risk the police.

I am sure they were immensely shocked. I think they expected a middle-aged suburban matron who would pass out; how were they to know they would get a banshee trained as a teacher in NSW secondary schools?

Of course the police weren't there.

My adrenalin was flowing like it hasn't for years. Underneath I was really quite frightened (and with good reason for the police said later that the glass door had been cut with a knife which they undoubtedly still had with them). Pippa was plain stunned. Having returned from the land of 'violence' she had been looking forward to some peace and quiet in the land of so-called civilised London. We needed more than one brandy to revive ourselves and to get things in perspective.

Then the police did arrive, and the CID, and the people to fix doors and walls, and it was all interruptions and there was no possibility of getting any work done. And on top of it all it was the first day of my period; never when I am at my best.

There was only one consolation; at least this time I didn't have to clean up the flat. Last time we were robbed it took a whole day to fix up the mess the robbers had made and two days (almost) to remove the magic dusting powder that the detectives had sprinkled liberally around in their search for fingerprints.

I suspect that such episodes – 'opportunistic' or 'casual' robbery the police call it – are going to become much more frequent in the future. It's a predictable 'side effect' of *male* unemployment. (Strange that no comment is made on the fact that it is only *one half* of the human species that responds in this way.) I must admit that there are occasions when I understand some of the feelings behind such 'anti-social' acts because it is pretty anti-social as far as I am concerned to define some members of society as superfluous or redundant. I have difficulty trying to decide whether it's more criminal to deliberately deprive a segment of the population of material resources and morale as the present government has done, or whether it's more criminal to 'hit back'.

Ted keeps telling me that it isn't that simple but I wish he wouldn't complicate my pure reasons and reasoning with his additional information. He maintains that he too would 'understand' if those who were doing the robbing were the ones the present government removed from the workforce, but it isn't always the case that robbers are 'unemployed'; some of them *choose* to be employed — as robbers, as far as he is concerned. He even has the hide to quote women as evidence — and declares quite openly that if unemployment led directly to robbery then there would be more women robbers than men. Personally I think I'll go back to my argument that milk is the source of all sin.

I used it the other day with a London cabbie — and as a result almost found myself walking home. He was complaining about 'crime' and told me that it was all because they had abolished capital punishment. I wasn't going to say anything but he kept asking me whether or not I agreed. So I said I thought it was the price of milk. That as far as I could see every time the price of milk went up, so too did the crime rate. I said I'd rather drop the price of milk than bring back the death penalty.

I don't know. When there's no more evidence that the death penalty will reduce the crime rate than a reduction in the price of milk, why is it that human beings can prefer killing to cheap milk? Sometimes I think there is probably something wrong with this world we live in.

By the way, I'm not surprised that Aaron has changed his name to Jim. Aaron is hardly a good Australian macho name and it had to change when some of his friends started to call him 'Airy' (in line with the other good Australian practice of adding 'ie' or 'y' as in 'cardie', 'kiddie' and 'mozzie' not to mention 'barbie', 'blowie', 'brecky' and 'bickie'). If he wanted the name of an Aussie hero it would have to be Jim . . . or Bill.

But I am interested in what you say about listening, . . . and 'Jim's' capacity not to. When I did the research of '*Man Made Language*' I basically believed that men did not hear when women spoke and that led to all those serious discussions about 'poor men' who didn't have listening skills and who needed extra attention to acquire them. Seems like just another trap to ensure that men get extra attention in my book. I've always been uncomfortable with the idea that boys are unable to listen when women talk and I think you have put your finger on the problem. It isn't that boys are *unable*, it is that they are *unavailable*. It's a cunning way of reinforcing their power isn't it? You only get heard when they are prepared to be available and as a women, *you* have to be *available* all the time. It makes women accountable on men's terms, and incidentally it does add credibility to the idea that women repeat themselves, that they nag and that they talk a lot. Patriarchy prevails.

I was sorry to hear that you birthday degenerated into decadence. If you are still suffering you have my sympathy. I know it must be hard for you with your puritanical streak to accept that the flesh is weak. You always were much happier when everyone else around you overindulged and you could do your sanctimonious bit. I can remember how you used to look at me morning after morning when I had a hangover and you were all fresh and healthy and bursting with energy. (It's why I can't bear the thought of you giving up smoking . . . you will make me feel weak and unclean in a matter of hours.)

Does age ever worry you? Can't say it worries me now. It used to, when I was trying so hard to be successfully feminine and when all the feminine assets *do* deteriorate with age . . . you have a right to be worried. But these days each year seems to be more affirming and I suppose I expect it to continue that way . . . until arthritis sets in. That's probably when I'll be on the first plane back to Australia for good. And you can push me round in my wheel chair to your heart's content (and scare shit out of me as I know you plan to do).

Sometimes I realise that I have an escape route that some of my English friends don't have and which probably gives me a different perspective on age. I always have at the back of my mind the picture of you and me as two old ladies in our tropical retreat, reading and writing and growing tomatoes. That's a slightly different picture from England in twenty or thirty years time, trying to live on the old age pension and travel on London buses ... with arthritis and a defunct National Health.

What do you think England will be like in twenty or thirty years? Are we seeing a developed country go over the top and into decline ... or will it become undeveloped? (Chicken or egg?) I was wondering about it the other night when I saw a great programme on telly. (Now that the bloody world soccer is over there are at least some programmes that I want to watch.)

The programme was on the Philippines and was amazing. The division there looks to be greater than it is here (yet), but the principle is much the same, with a small group of obscenely wealthy 'haves' (primarily the president and his first lady plus assorted relatives I think), and a vast number of 'have-nots'. Seventy per cent of the children suffered from malnutrition in a country that could feed itself – and more – and it seems that the main reason behind the 'mismanagement' is, (can you guess?) ... US influence!

US militarism (evidently the Philippines are strategically important) means a huge influx of weapons and lethal paraphernalia and as there is no 'enemy', it is a simple matter to use it against the local population and to create a police state. And US economists want a safe haven for 'investment' so instead of feeding the country you have *development*, with local fishermen forced out of their waters to make way for the multinational fish processing factories which can make such good use of the abundance of 'cheap labour'.

At the beginning, the programme was drainingly depressing but it soon introduced a twist that was dear to my heart. It moved out of the urban slums and to the rice fields, and apart from showing some of the most stunning scenery, with levels of rice farming down a mountainside, there were also interviews with the people ... who were fascinating.

Village life was simple but according to the people who lived there, it had no problems which couldn't be solved by the presence of a few more barefoot doctors. But village life was about to be eliminated to make way for a hydro-electric power scheme ˙. . . which would of course provide cheap power to go with the cheap labour and help constitute a multi-national paradise. The rice growers were just supposed to get up and leave . . . in the name of progress and more jobs and better quality of life! Whole communities which had been there for generation after generation were supposed to abandon their land, their self-sufficient way of life, their heritage . . . and supposedly just disappear, so the country could be developed.

And the people were so sensible and sophisticated. No reverence for technology. They absolutely scorned the notion of being 'developed' and it is the first time I have heard such sound and caustic arguments about why anyone would choose to be developed. In the minds of the interviewers (and I suspect the viewers at home), the idea of progress and industrial development is so taken for granted as a good thing that questions about its advantages and disadvantages are virtually never raised. The assumption is that the undeveloped world is eagerly waiting to be developed . . . and here were all these people loudly and logically dismissing development as ludicrous.

Are you advertising the developed world as paradise, they demanded to know? And part of the programme looked at the imported, developed, American culture. And through their eyes it just looked so awful. There were scenes of towns that had been turned into rest and recreation centres for the American Seventh Fleet . . . all reminiscent of Saigon . . . brawls, drunkenness, massage parlours, prostitutes, pornography . . . dreadful. Belligerence and dominance and decadence as well. Some of the villagers were angered and hurt by the Filipino singers who were emulating western rock and punk and they felt as vehemently about the colonisation of their minds as they did about the colonisation of their rice fields.

I'm not trying to suggest that there was a rural idyll about to be spoiled . . . obviously there were aspects of the rice growers'

lives that were hard – and they all wished they had more
medical advances . . . but not the great technological marvels of
the new heart hospital for the wealthy . . . they wanted to deal
more effectively with gastro-enteritis and dysentery. But there
was no denying that they had food and shelter and leisure and
dignity and *meaning*, and *they* didn't think they were undeveloped, deprived, or deserving of pity and patronage! On the
contrary, they were adamant that it would be if they *were*
developed that they would be in need. They would then have
no means of living, no place to go. And all this 'progress' – and
pain – in the interest of lining the president's pocket.

They didn't really know how to go about preventing
development (and undermining the police state). The man who
presented the programme seemed to spend a lot of his life in jail
. . . along with his friends. I suppose it is something of a miracle
that the programme could even be made, and shown in Britain.
And one of the pleas that was made in it was for the British to
register protests with the government about US involvement in
the Philippines, about the US human rights record there, and
its colonisation and exploitation.

No doubt that will be sufficient for it to be considered
unsuitable viewing in Australia, so you'll probably never get to
see it. For an Asian country, Australians know next to nothing
about Asia. Could probably register a protest about the US
colonisation of Australia . . . and Australian minds. I've learnt
more about places like the Philippines and India since I have
lived here than I ever did in Australia . . . and of course much
more that is critical of the US.

It's a pretty depressing world isn't it? Even if there are
occasional groups who spurn the idea of development and seek
only barefoot doctors (you can see that they would never be
successful consumers and supporters of the capitalist state with
that mentality). There are times when I cannot bring myself to
think about what the outcome will be. The chances of us all
being blown up (with the exception of those who make the
decisions, push the buttons and have their bunkers well
organised) are growing greater and greater. In a way I almost
wish there were some signs of the economists getting it right

and delivering us from the depression – for what I do know is that in the past the standard solution to unemployment has been war, and with so much unemployment now in so many countries, I suspect that the war solution is gaining in momentum.

In this context there are times when I feel pretty silly. How can I justifiably continue to write about Hazel (Hunkins Hallinan) and Mary Stott (the sections on them are going well and are almost complete) when life and death issues surround me? How can I plan what books I will write next year when the overriding question is whether there will be a next year? I get so uneasy about what I am doing and why. It seems so self indulgent, so 'trivial'. There are days when I can sustain my thesis that writing is a political act, that it is important for people to have information . . . but sometimes it is hard work trying to maintain that line. I think of how privileged I am and ask myself what I am doing with the resources which I didn't earn, but which have been granted to me as a white Westerner.

And then it all gets too much and I think of the futility of being depressed . . . and react. And decide that there should be something that is a bright spot in the bleak world. I think that is the mood I was in when I drafted the proposal the other night for a new book. *'Join the Women's Movement and Improve Your IQ'.* Could even offer a money back guarantee. Do you think Robyn would design an IQ test for me where feminists scored higher than non-feminists? Shouldn't be hard . . . psychologists have been designing selective intelligence tests for years. It's our turn now, though.

Good Goddess! (to coin a phrase). What are you going to do about life in London? What with robbers, the demise of your local wine bar and the imminent approach of winter, it is almost enough to make you want to return to Australia. Do keep in mind though, that here we have 'burglars' whose numbers will no doubt increase along with unemployment (which is, as any good economist will tell you, an unavoidable side-effect of every anti-inflation policy.) And here don't forget, we do not have local wine bars to undergo a decline. All appropriate sites are already occupied by pubs of the hose-out-at-night variety or by clubs which are decorated in the interior with thousands of poker machines – all of which are monuments to the importance of 'male members'. More phallic cultural artifacts I have only seen in Greece, on the now uninhabited islands, where huge, carved penises have fallen to the ground in what should be a demonstration to all the world of what happens when you take men seriously . . . or more importantly, when you let them *take* each other – seriously!

Really though, the robber experience must have been awful. Even so, I would have liked to witness it and I assure you that I can imagine your language. We are not 'wild colonials' for nothing. I gather that you think you have overcome your female conditioning and the learned inability to lash out physically. I know that women who teach self-defence maintain that the most difficult thing for women to learn is to give themselves permission to aim their blows where they will hurt most. I remember thinking, in line with my theory that women's antipathy to sex was a 'natural' contraceptive, that male genital vulnerability was a 'natural' form of protection for women. But we are taught that it is unfair to 'hit below the belt' (the only chance we have when face-to-face) just as it's not fair to hit a man from behind (our only other chance when they weigh so much more than we do). You know who made up those rules, don't you? They're even encoded in the law. Thus, with their greater body weight, men can kill women with one angry blow and get away with a charge of manslaughter (no rules about below the belt) while a woman in a recent case in south Australia (who had been periodically beaten by her husband for years), retaliated by hitting him when he was asleep and copped the full force of the law and pre-meditated murder. For the same crime of one person killing another, the woman receives a far greater penalty because men made up the laws to cover themselves. Even though her reasons are more 'reasonable', her offence is seen as more serious. And I've no doubt it appears that way to men. That's male justice. It doesn't have much claim though as a 'universal' system of justice.

Talking of 'justice', I had to play magistrate in charge of summary offences yesterday. Aaron (still Jim to his friends) decided that he wanted to make some chocolate crackles – you know those chocolate covered rice bubbles – and he painstakingly measured and mixed his ingredients to produce twenty or so of those very messy, but I must admit, very tasty, treats. While they were setting in the fridge and he was out playing, his elder brother of whom I am becoming less fond by the hour, discovered the crackles and with several of his friends, sold them at the football oval for twenty cents each. Now, had they returned and distributed their profits according to *my* idea of justice – that is, giving Jim a larger share to compensate him for his hard work, all may have been well. However, the money-making syndicate totally excluded Jim from the end of day accounting and profit-sharing. They retired to the 'cubby' (which they built in and around my favourite plants) and very loudly counted *their* loot while Jim howled and screamed outside the makeshift cubby door.

Chief Justice Lou was obliged to preside over the ensuing proceeding as a *non*-stipendiary magistrate and eventually gave up trying to convince the hardened offenders of the error of their ways. The end result was that they did agree to share the profits equally (many arguments that as Jim was smaller, he should get less) and the only person who really missed out was me. I was left to clean up the cleaning-up after the crackles were made, to replace the ingredients used and to try and save the several plants that were trampled during the hearing – if not before. Oh, I forgot – I was also left with the delight and rewards of raising two beautiful children. I wonder when the rewards will come!

Thank you for your sympathetic comments about my birthday celebrations. I assume that you are still harbouring resentment about the article on snoring that I sent you or you would not have felt obliged to add the totally unnecessary (even if relevant) references to my puritanical/sanctimonious streak. I felt quite bad enough without your pointing out that my strategies are so transparent.

About age! It's not something that I give much credibility to in my daily routine – I don't have time – and like you, in a general sense I feel each year brings more rather than takes something away. I am, however, sometimes aware that my physical sense of self is not quite as positive as it used to be. I always did have a greater investment than you in the 'body' (no doubt directly attributable to the unwanted and disturbing growth of larger than average boobs during my adolescence). I'm sure my sense of infallibility about child-birth was related to an absolute faith in my fit and healthy body and perhaps the negative experiences in that context introduced a few doubts. I'm not sure of the origins, but there are now times when I prefer to place my faith in the abilities of mind rather than the body. I suppose that's ageing. It's certainly a reflection of a culture that separate the mind and the body into two different entities (how absurd) and which, as far as women are concerned, places more emphasis on the body. Like you though, I have a security that sisterless women don't often have. I assure you that when we retire, while I may mock your tendency to snore and you may chide me for my puritanism, neither of us will reject the other because of wrinkles or sagging breasts!

Your observations about the programme on the Philippines struck quite a chord here. Sue and I were having a discussion this week about women in third World Countries because she is doing a unit on Women and Development in the MA Course. She was disturbed that initial discussions in the course revealed a total acceptance of the hierarchy involved in labelling countries 'first', 'second' and 'third' world. She was also aware that few of the other people doing the course could easily accept that *education*, as we know it, might not only be useless to women in those societies, it might actually be harmful. We realized that so many of us take it for granted that our ways are 'better' and that we have a missionary-like obligation to 'improve' and 'aid' others so that they can be like us. Yet, it doesn't take much to understand that in the Philippine context, the 'development' that is being imposed is awful and that the education that we could offer women would inevitably reflect our society's attitude towards women as inferior. The end result must be to deprive women of their current status and to replace it with an inferior one *and* without the tools to engage in the battles that we as feminists are still fighting here. I can understand how those with economic interests in development can totally ignore this dimension but you would think that the 'do-gooders' at least would have learned something from the terrible mistakes made by the Christian missionaries. Perhaps, as you point out, people here may not even be aware of the issues involved. Programmes like the one on the Philippines are not valued much here and if they are shown it is on a Sunday afternoon when all 'thinking' Australians are either at the football or watching it on the 'other' channel. In fact, Australian TV seems to perform quite a different function from that of the BBC. The rationale here is for TV as entertainment rather than as information or intellectual simulation. The commercial channels set the scene and the ABC does an uncomfortable compromise competing with the commercial channels during peak viewing hours with 'entertaining' prog-rammes and offering its informational programmes when no-one watches TV. I can only assume that it is all part of a wider 'plot' against the development of Australian intelligence. It is so much easier to manipulate people when they are uninformed or misinformed . . . ask any feminist!

On a more amusing note, I thought you might like a personal anecdote from the antipodes. Sue and I met in town during the week to have our annual pap-smears (free at the VD clinic) and witnessed two young women who came to the realization 'before our very eyes' that they had been sleeping with the same man – and neither knew of the existence of the other. I had a great deal of trouble trying not to laugh (it's not funny!) and delighted in eavesdropping on the plans they were making to expose the culprit. Among other more personal actions, they were going to put his name on the noticeboard at the office where they worked stating that he was a carrier of a communicable venereal disease. Christabel Pankhurst must have been smiling. 'VOTES FOR WOMEN AND CHASTITY FOR MEN'. It still holds true. There was another female there who was outraged that the doctor (male) had inferred that vaginal discharge was directly connected with a lack of heterosexual sex and resulted in 'pelvic congestion'. How's that for reflecting men at twice their normal size? Apparently, if we don't make ourselves sexually available, our bodies will rebel or congest. It did occur to me that most *women* would probably connect vaginal discharge *with* sexual activity rather than with a lack of it.

You ask in your letter (which I received this morning) what I think England will be like in twenty years time. There are several possible scenarios – none of which particularly appeals to my sense of order and well-being. The first is that it may well be totally destroyed by nuclear acitivty. That scenario is no longer just a vague fear in the minds of the radical few but a very real possibility and I, like many others, find myself almost obliged to ignore it in order to put some meaning into my daily existence. Obviously, you feel a bit the same way. What is the point in planning next year's books or for that matter worrying about the children's moral development when we don't even know if we'll be here next year. Why is it that the two-faced, male face of politics refuses to deal with this possibility as an issue. I suppose it's to save face. (Pardon the puns! I didn't notice.)

The second scenario that I can imagine is one where so many people will be reduced to abject poverty that capitalism will again have a cheap and manipulable labour force available for exploitation. I am quite convinced that one aspect of the current economic recession relates to the fact that Western countries (the States particularly) have run out of 'third world' populations to exploit and as one of the by-products of capitalism is undoubtedly a rise in the expectations and living standards of its workers, it is having to return to home ground and recreate its own, large group of workers who will work for next to nothing and give the capitalist economy time to rationalise, restructure and start the whole process all over again – but this time with technology as its magic wand. *The* (London) *Times* will rise again like a phoenix from the ashes and there will be no more trouble for quite some time either with workers who refuse to utilize the new technology (so that they will become redundant) or journalists who refuse to present the 'party line' to the public. It's quite simple really. Just a matter of a few strokes of the pen and a little time and approximately half the population of England out of work.

The third picture that I can see is the only one that offers any hope to any more than the few at the top and it is England as a product of the 'revolution' amongst women. A combination of Zoë's *'Benefits'** and Charlotte Perkins Gilman's *'Herland'*. I realise that envisaging a feminist future leaves one very open to ridicule and contempt – what do we have to offer in the way of proven policies and practice? Absolutely nothing in the political context. As with education, men have made fairly sure that we are deprived of the qualities and opportunities that they see as essential for 'management'. Thus they can turn around and

---

* Zoë Fairbairns, *'Benefits'*, Virago Press, London 1979.

criticise us for not having them. But as Mary O'Brien in Canada used to say – we do have something that men no longer have – if they had it at all. We do have a vision of how things *could* work to benefit all instead of just the few (sounds a bit like the 'dreaded reds' doesn't it?), and we do have an understanding of the on-going quality of life. All those women out there who have raised and been responsible for kids, who have managed their families on the basis of tomorrow and tomorrow, rather than today. All of them understand at a gut level what it means to plan, to negotiate and to accommodate, so that life goes on with some human meaning. My first act as mistress in charge of big boys would be to get them out to dig up all the football fields (where currently children aren't allowed to play and even have to pay money to *watch* the big boys play) and to turn them into vegetable gardens. Every community would thus have a supply of food and the big boys would get their exercise and their opportunities for camaraderie while they hoed the fields. After they had done adequate exercise for the day (I wouldn't want to exploit them) they could get clean and dressed up and the prettiest ones could deliver the produce to those in most need of it. Thus they, the big boys, could provide both the food and the delivery service and provide too, some pleasure for those of us who appreciate beauty in any form. Do you want more? I could go on . . .

Why do you have to present such contrasting pictures of England in twenty or thirty years time? Talk about learning to live with contradictions – I didn't know whether to be relieved that we might not have a future (and I agree with your sound economic analysis that capitalism is now 'bringing it all back home') or to be pleased at the prospect of the pretty boys delivering produce to the needy – grown with their own hands on their own fertile football fields. Now that's the future I fancy!

It seems to me that the most 'sci-fi' you can get these days is to assume there will be a future. I was sorting through some recent press cuttings yesterday (as a prelude to doing some filing and finishing with a tidy desk . . . and I'll be pleased to pass on any pointers you may need), and found one called 'War on Peace Studies'. I don't know whether it is serious or a spoof but then as a humourless feminist my judgement in these matters is definitely unreliable. It's from *The Observer* and begins with the statement that the government is becoming anxious at the growing popularity of political education and peace studies in schools and colleges. Well, I suppose one should be thankful for small mercies . . . and take solace in the fact that peace studies and politics are finally being linked. But you should see how it goes on. The Education Authorities are being attacked for permiting *appeasement* studies in schools. (Now there's an unemotive and neutral term for you.) 'Politics' said Dr Rhodes Boyson, 'like sex education, is something that should be left to the family. Schools can just become a depository for all the problems that society doesn't know what to do about.'

Now I should have thought that the unsolved problems of society were precisely those areas which demanded attention in our halls of learning, but then I am not Dr Rhodes Boyson (and I must point out to some of my aspiring PhD friends that he gained membership to the exclusive club), and the junior education minister.

Here we go again. Virginia Woolf went through all this in 'Three Guineas' (1938 . . . we are a bit early if it is every fifty years that women reinvent the wheel). Her book was devoted to the thesis that education in our society is education for war, and that women therefore, have a moral duty to stay outside education in the interests of peace. From football fields to examination results and professional occupations she insisted that the underlying motive was conquest and that the products of our education system were only fit for confrontation, for solving problems by force. And I'd say it is still the same. But the wise man sees nothing political or offensive in this education system which confirms his view of the natural world. And the wise woman who is an outsider and sees something very different? Well, we all know what happened to wise women . . . they were burnt at the stake.

Am I locked into a single frame of reference or is it that there is a single, simple explanation behind these apparent absurdities? It seems that everywhere I look it comes down to *power*, with those who have the power calling their world the natural and neutral order and branding as treacherous to insane anyone who disagrees. Is this where human intelligence has led us?

Those in power can forcefully insist on their own objectivity and cool calm reason (and hard facts) while they lay the foundation stones of making dirty words out of *Peace, Conciliation, Appeasement, Co-operation*. After that, it is a pretty easy matter to deride and dismiss those who are associated with such terrible qualities. It's but a small step to make the women who identify with peace or cooperation look anything from errant to evil.

Come back Matilda Joslyn Gage and give them a piece of your mind. I promise you men like Rhodes Boyson would be excellent material for your thesis on the ungovernable frenzy of the male. (By the way what are the rules for libel/defamation when it comes to these letters? I wouldn't want to be sued by someone like Rhodes Boyson. Knowing what he thinks of peace educators I can hardly bring myself to examine his attitude towards home-destroying, man-hating, embittered feminists. And apart from that, as you point out, the courts have been made by men for men so I don't think it would be too rash of us to predict that if I were sued, I would not win.)

Just how far are you into your legal studies anyway? A distinct legal dimension is emerging in your arguments and metaphors. I'm not quite sure what a *non*-stipendiary magistrate is, but as stipend means pay, I assume the *non*-Stipendiary magistrates are the ones who are *unpaid* for their works, and are therefore female. Is that right?

Linguistic difficulties aside, I did feel considerable sympathy for 'Jim' and the way he was deprived of his resources when it came to the episode of the chocolate crackles. I am sure that you would have taken the opportunity to point out to him that such a dreadful fate befalls many women every day as they make much more than chocolate crackles, and their efforts are appropriated by males who proceed to sell their energy for cash which they dispose of without reference to the women who made it all possible.

And I don't think there is any necessity to teach Jay the fundamental principles of capitalism – on the contrary it sounds as though he could already give you and me some lessons. (I have no recollections of us exploiting each other in comparable ways in our youth – have I a selective memory or is it that we really are either honourable . . . or stupid?)

You can tell Jay that after this he has almost convinced me that there is something in the doctrine of original sin. I'll leave you to provide the explanations and to find favour with Rhodes Boyson by keeping it in the home. I can't bring myself to face another of those painful correspondences with Jay where in his very large and wobbly printing (which I know in part I am responsible for by telling him that it didn't matter . . . no one would ask him what his printing was like when he was an adult), he kept sending me letters that demanded to know *what I meant*. Do you remember when he sent me a letter saying that if I wasn't good to god he would punish me . . . by giving me nothing but pumpkin to eat for one whole year? And I wrote back and told him not to be silly, that even if god wanted to be spiteful, and mean and nasty, his mother wouldn't let him! That exchange went on for months and was exhausting.

But perhaps you shouldn't convey the message to him. And it isn't really you I am thinking of. Jay gets enough 'negative feedback' from school as it is. It's strange how our feminist sense of humour is rarely appreciated by his teachers.

Not that I would expect to be appreciated by authority figures of course. If society started to understand that when men mock women it's called a joke and when women mock men it's called manhating, I'd lose one of my wittiest ways of pointing out that men are in charge of the value system.

I had one of the most delicious evenings ever during the week when I went to see Victoria Wood (who, in case you have forgotten, is one of those rare species while men decide what is funny and what is not . . . a comedienne). I can't tell you how 'esteeming', energising and entertaining it was to have a woman's jokes about women and men. There were jokes about upper class ladies and hand embroidered tampons, about adult education classes in coping with cystitis and there were subversive and satirical songs about sexual intercourse – and why doesn't Barbara Cartland write stories about love between dykes? There was also a beautiful ballad about taking the piss out of men.

But from some of the facial expressions of the men it was quite clear that this was nothing but more evidence that women had no sense of humour. (In contrast to many of the men there were women falling about themselves with laughter . . . and providing another example as far as the men were concerned that there really is something wrong with women.) I'm sure it is not just that the men were made uncomfortable with all the talk about tampons and sanitary napkins, it really was that they didn't understand the point of the humour.

I suppose if humour does depend on juxtaposition and incongruity then you have to know about tampons (among other things) to see the incongruity and to appreciate the joke. And of course so many men – even among the liberated – do not know about the 'intimate' aspects of female existence . . . and no prizes for guessing who draws the boundary line and decides what's intimate. And while the boundary line and the taboo prevails . . . and it still isn't done to talk about tampons in public (public being men of course), then men won't find out, will they?

Sometimes I think about risk-taking in this area and about doing something to make women's reality more public. It would just be in the name of social advancement you understand. A couple of times in mixed sex company when I have been told I look tired or something. I have proffered the information that I have my period. And on more than one occasion I have produced a tampon from my handbag . . . not always intentionally, I have at times mistaken it for my lipsalve when burrowing in the depths of my bag . . . but the shock/horror/embarrassment is too much to take. You do feel a bit like a leper when everyone round lowers their eyes, looks away, coughs and changes the conversation. It's hard to preserve the facade of confidence and to maintain the belief that you have done nothing criminal by drawing attention to the reality of a quarter of the adult women in the room. It will take a braver person than I am, I'm afraid to tackle that little problem.

It is one of the reasons I have so much admiration for Christabel (Pankhurst) who in the words of Rebecca West performed one of the greatest services for women's liberation when she persisted in speaking so loudly and in *the worst possible taste* about venereal disease. She broke the taboo and helped to make women's pain . . . and ignorance . . . a topic; after that women's experience of venereal disease was 'speakable about' and it just wasn't possible to go on as if it didn't exist. I do think someone has got to *publicly* expose comparable areas today . . . and humour is a good way of doing it.

After all there are some aspects of women's reality that are hilariously funny. I've never heard a discussion about 'My first day with a tampon' that hasn't reduced me to helpless laughter . . . but such discussion are always 'women only'. (Remember our mutual friend who kept insisting that she didn't have a hole, and our growing impatience and practical instruction? And then later the medical opinion that indeed she was not endowed with such a facility.)

Humour does tend to take the edge off pain and anger and it certainly provides a positive way of dealing with difficulties. I think we should have much more of it.

Since all this toxic shock sensation I find I am reluctant to use tampons – but the alternative of sanitary napkins just presents so many problems. I can tell you without a shadow of a doubt that women have neither designed nor equipped the majority of toilet facilities (in public or private places) in this city so again and again that dreadful problem arises; short of causing plumbing pandemonium (as schoolgirls are wont to do), or wrapping it in one's handbag, what is one to do? (And besides with my record with handbags I have good reason to worry about that as a solution.) After the event there is always a way of making an amusing episode from it . . . but at the time it is just another wretched reminder that the world is run by and for men.

I am sure you can vividly recall that time you took to flight with your new born babe and found that in aeroplane and airport the only place for *him* when *you* wanted to pee, was on the lavatory floor. Being introduced to germs so early and so thoroughly doesn't seem to have done him any harm though . . . see, that is what happens, that's sort-of-making a joke out of it. But you laughed little at the time. I think he still represented so much 'effort' on your part that any potential threat to him was viewed with martyrish horror.

So much of women's lives get left out of social consciousness and yet it is known in such detail to women. A woman from Cambridge was chatting to me the other day about not being able to cope with life in London and she asked me 'What about the tubes?'. I knew straight away the question was about deserted and poorly lit tunnels and the fear of attack but I am sure most men would have been mystified both by the question and the answer. But every women would have known instantly what sort of meanings were being exchanged.

At times it seems so simple . . . women and men inhabit such different worlds that the same incident can mean something dramatically different depending on whether one is female or male . . . yet so many people go on as if it is a single order world, where there is only one meaning. When I talk about this (in public) I'm often asked in the most belligerent fashion to give an example of the same event meaning entirely different things and the first one that usually comes to mind is rape – the rapist and the raped could hardly be said to be participating in the same event. I suppose you could include wife beating in that too.

I have used illegitimacy as well, and argued that it is a concept that only men could have generated. No woman is going to give birth and gaze at the child and ask whether it is 'legitimate', or indeed, whether it is hers!

But Robyn's (Rowland) analysis of *power* is still probably the most sensational in the response it provokes and I'll always be grateful to her for that particular gem. I used it last week in a lecture as an illustration and the women were overcome with laughter and two men actually got up, glared at me, and stalked out. I did enjoy it.

I pointed out that if tomorrow all the women in Camden Town withheld all sexual favours from men until the streets in the area were properly lit and patrolled by women police, then it was likely that something would soon be done to make the streets safer for women. But the same *power* is not held by men. We don't talk of men granting sexual favours. If all the men decided tomorrow to withhold their sexual favours . . . most women would probably be quite relieved. It wouldn't be a bargaining position for men.

There was a lot of recognition and relief in the women's laughter. I'm still struck by the fact that in private so many women indicate that sex is not a source of satisfaction to them and yet publicly the 'full orgasmic life' faces few challenges and has few critics. We do *conform* don't we? If this is sexual liberation, what was sexual oppression?

After the laughter had subsided in the lecture theatre I got round to talking about women's sexual autonomy and I could see that there were a few women entertaining theoretical possibilities. Of course in our sexually saturated society I suspect most of them were thinking in terms of masturbation because the possibility that you don't *need* sex to survive is not one that rushes to the forefront of consciousness. (I refuse to use the word 'celibacy' because it implies *denial* and is but the reverse side of the belief that sex is essential and that it is possible to be deprived of it.) I don't suppose I should be surprised that there isn't a word in the English language to encompass what I do mean. It's like walking through a linguistic minefield in today's terms if you want to suggest some alternative to our present sex compulsions. But I am sure that even without the word, you know precisely what I mean. Boycott, non-consumption, non-cooperation with the ideology makers?

Not knowing that it was necessary for 'full development' there were so many nineteenth-century women who felt neither deprived nor disturbed by the absence of heterosexual inter-course and I am sure that they would understand as well what I am talking about. No doubt they would even be astonished if they came back today and found that you were expected to explode or dwindle without a full sex life; they would have to acknowledge that human beings had evolved remarkably in a very short space of time.

Even good old Karl Marx would probably have a fit and revise his words of wisdom from *religion* is the opiate of the people, to *orgasm* is the opiate of the people. The conventional wisdom suggests that the material conditions are of no consequence as long as the 'sex' is good. How often have you heard a woman protesting about the viciousness of her life with a certain man only to be asked, 'Is the sex good?'.

If I keep going on this track I'll get more and more depressed and I've got enough *real* things . . . already given good old

English words . . . to make me depressed without adding to it. Like *post*. I'll go bananas soon. It grows and grows no matter how much time I spend on it. As more women are becoming unemployed more of them are writing more job applications and asking me to be a referee. I can't say NO. I don't want to say no, but there's no point in writing a reference unless you take some time and care with it – better not to do it at all than to write two non-committal and superficial paragraphs. But it takes more than a day a week now to get through them. And while I write references, I don't write books.

I'm trying to get '*There's Always Been a Women's Movement*' finished before I go on holidays . . . although part of me admits already that such a goal is totally unrealistic. But the days I can get up and start writing from early in the morning and keep at it until after midnight are the most satisfying ones of my life. I wouldn't want to do that seven days a week (I might, you know), but I very much want to do it three or four days a week. Two uninterrupted days in my writing room (ignoring the post) and I have another fifty pages done.

The only problem with that is that if I do keep at it five days a week I write a book a month and apart from the fact that publishers don't seem to be able to process contracts in less than six months (which would mean that I would have a stack of uncontracted, unpublished manuscripts . . . think of that in contrast to racing to meet deadlines) there is also the sinking fear that *I might run out of things to say.*

I've got six probables at gestation stage at the moment so at my present rate of progress I'm probably safe for another two years. (I'll send you the outlines when I type them up.) But I can't do any of them while I am on holiday . . . because they all need bloody reference books and articles etc. And I'm blowed if I will set out for a holiday in the sun weighed down by reference books.

So have been thinking of whether or not to try my hand at fiction, or drama. I can do that with just pen and paper. Already I'm starting to worry (as you can see) about what I shall do for two weeks. Ted looks forward to the sheer mindlessness of sleeping and eating but you know I can only take a couple of days of that. I'm getting panicky . . . and I face the fact of course that I can't carry enough books to read . . . even if there were enough published in the next few weeks which I wanted to read. (Ted has bought a number of books and hidden them from me to be produced when we get there. Chocolate and books, both my weaknesses and both elicit the same response . . . if they are there I consume them. Hence Ted's habit of stocking up and producing a pile at the appropriate moment. He dreads more than I do I think the prospect of me running out of reading matter.)

So what do you think about some fiction writing? Do you think I could do it? Should do it? I'd dearly love to write a feminist thriller and while part of me says it can't be that difficult, and of course you can do it, (the very advice I am always handing out so liberally to others), another part says *you can't*! The fear of the unfamiliar. But it would be a solution as far as the holiday goes. If I get sick of the sun, or run out of reading, I can experiment with the writing.

Sounds sensible . . . and terrifying! Maybe I should just stay home (and answer the post). But my now curved spine needs to be supine for a few days. Is this middle age, and occupational hazard, or the (English) dreaded arthritis?

✒ Coogee, August 1982

Am 'sneaking' some time while the children are in their room watching a hideous television programme which I am prepared to criticise vehemently *and* to allow them to watch. Rather a contradiction, I suppose, but as I have mentioned before, there comes a˙time in every woman's life when she must decide whether to put her energy into herself or into others and tonight, this woman has decided in favour of self. On the basis of rational decision-making processes, I have determined –

(a) that the children have years ahead to pursue their own interests while I have spent years unable to follow mine.
(b) that I resent feeling that I ought to stand between them and the TV world of violence and sexism. Who decided that the moral development of the next generation was to devolve onto *female* parents?
(c) that I can't be bothered finding and presenting the three reasonable arguments that they will insist I provide (according to democratic principles) if I am really committed to the idea that children are people too.

Apart from those careful rationalisations, I have a great deal to 'talk' to you about and can see absolutely no reason why they should interfere with the discussion.

So there!

I had the rather frightening experience last weekend of attending a 'youthful' party (under 25s) and of witnessing the Australian version of how men *do* dominate in social situations. There were several couples there and within the first half-hour, I (and everyone else) saw two of the young men (who are, by the way, the up-and-coming professionals of the next generation), totally dismiss the opinions and comments of their female partners. One did it in the loving and protective style 'You silly girl – what would you know about it?' (accompanied by a nibble on the left ear lobe) and the other became quite irritated that his partner felt entitled to speak on *his* subject – 'I have done the degree – you only typed the thesis!'

Not surprisingly, I did not hear from either of those two young women for the rest of the evening. One became more 'child-like' with each drink and eventually had to be taken home to bed, and the other withdrew into what I assumed was a marijuana-induced state of protected privacy. Meanwhile, the dashing and intelligent young men pursued their conversations with their true peers who seem to be men their own age and women who are at least 5-10 years older. I can only conclude that in this country for women to be equal to men, they not only have to be better but at least five years older. I suppose the idea is that an extra few years experience of the world can compensate for their 'natural' deficiencies. Whatever the explanation, it seems fairly clear that Australian men want to have their 'wives' sitting silently at their sides while they avail themselves of other women who may have either intellectual or other resources to offer them. Thanks to information provided by Matilda Joslyn Gage 100 years ago, I have no doubt that the men appropriated what they learned from the older women and used it not only to impress their male colleagues but to demonstrate to their wives that there are divisions between 'wives' and 'women' and that wives should not challenge their husbands in social situations. While children are learning to be people, it would seem that wives are learning to be children and should be 'seen and not heard'. And

I was beginning to think that there was some hope of change embodied in the future generation!

Item 2

I am a little surprised that you are surprised by the reaction to *appeasement* studies in schools. I suppose it is the blatant display of sexual politics that is so distressing. But no-one who has survived the current education system with thinking powers still intact has any concept of schools being 'halls of learning'. They are not meant to be places where *new* ideas and strategies are tested or put into practice. Good Goddess! Any one such idea might prove popular or even workable and could result in the overthrow of the establishment and of people like your 'Dr Whatsit' who heads up the resistance movement. That's revolution! Halls of learning are meant to be places where we admire – without touching – what men have done and said in the past – a bit like museums. Their other function is to keep young and active minds 'contained', preferably at hours that are most inconvenient for mothers who have to work to support them. Imagine what children might learn if they were allowed to explore the world outside the halls of learning. Or better, imagine what they would *not* learn? Who would teach them about the glories of war or that the virtues of competition and conquest are all that differentiate *man* from nature (i.e. the rest of the world, including women). And imagine what women might do if they did not feel obliged to provide before and after school care for their children. They might want to compete with men for full-time jobs. It would be just like women to want to have everything and to take jobs away from men. No. Better that children have malnutrition and their mums at home to look after them than to risk any alteration to the system, It's obviously much more reasonable to have men exempted from the onerous task of child-care so that they can be free to make money while the halls of learning teach children that men have got it right. To teach *peace* or to change the present structure of the schools, would be to come face to face with the fact that past and present, men have frequently got it wrong.

My own experience in the halls of learning this week (which

153

you may have guessed lay behind the previous diatribe) have not been particularly rewarding. The more I read law, the more I realise that I am in fact reading about men's good opinion of themselves. Our learned legal forefathers went to quite incredible lengths to protect themselves and each other and in doing so established the 'precedents' that we still follow today as the correct stating of the common law. Only when some of the privileges of the rich and well-educated have been threatened has there been any change in the 'correct' stating of the law – and as the rich and well-educated still tend to be the male of the species, it is not surprising that the majority of decisions from as far back as the seventeenth century are today seen as relevant and worth upholding. Of course, such decisions are explained in terms of a moral and un-changing notion of justice and are thus removed from men's personal interests, but for one who knows about rationalising (the children *are* still watching that awful show) it's rather hollow. A demonstration that the halls of learning are meant to preserve the status quo and not change it.

Meanwhile, in the 'other place', I find myself being equally frustrated by a course in Women's Studies that has no guiding philosophy, and for which tutors have been selected on the basis of economic expediency rather than any understanding of or commitment to women. I am delighted that Women's Studies is being offered at post-graduate level but am also troubled by the fact that what W.S. means to most people here is studying what amounts to men's poor opinion of women. It is merely ingesting and regurgitating the established body of man-made knowledge about women. The end result will be either that W.S. fades out for women because it is so depressing and so far removed from their experience or that it will flourish and attract a male head of department because he is an expert on why there have been no great women writers, artists or women's studies students . . . I really am torn between rejoicing at the existence of the course and despairing that the course should consist of a static body of knowledge which can be 'taught', 'learned' – even by men – and which may never challenge any of the fundamental patriarchal ploys. I would love to write a critique of the course but know it would be used against women and would probably be the impetus for the university to send in a few males to 'sweep the floor clean'. Thank heavens I can talk about it to you. If I couldn't, I think I would be in danger of losing sight of some of my feminist beliefs and ideals. I would certainly be in danger of losing my 'rational' mind.

Item 3

Made the effort financially and time-wise to see David Williamson's new play, '*The Perfectionist*' at the Opera House during the week. Had the dubious experience of getting a 'standing' seat ($6.80 compared to $15.00) and stood at the back of the theatre, behind the booked seats (some of which were empty) and was 'entertained' by a man's idea of contemporary heterosexual relationships as influenced by feminism. Apart from the fact that I was well aware of some of the reasons behind the French Revolution – having to stand while the wealthy few sat in luxury – I was also very aware of the way Williamson had picked up on quite a bit of feminist ideology and had turned it around so that it was presented as just another passing fad, like hippiedom, that had its attractions but which ultimately worked against the *real* and *natural* male-as-dominant-relationship between couples. Basically, the story of a marriage where husband and wife are both doing PhDs and where Williamson makes it quite clear that the man sees *his* study as far more important than *hers* and that in spite of the fact that he is a sensitive, kind and loving father, child-care is also *her* responsibility. The dialogue made that point quite well but unfortunately the play itself reaffirmed the idea that he was probably justified in assuming his role to be more important. If their roles are to be given equal importance, it is just asking for trouble. Implied was the idea that one of them has to give way and for the sake of tradition and convenience, it may as well be her. There was no credibility given to the feminist notions that change might be positive – for both sexes – and I imagine that the 250 couples in attendance at the play (seated) went home thinking that what they had was all they could expect.

'Thank heavens for our miserable relationship. Look how bad it could be if feminists were in control.' I had a sneaking suspicion that David Williamson had read some reviews of Betty Friedan's the '*Second Stage*' and had decided that he would be on the bandwagon for the demise of feminism. It is definitely part of the plot!

Item 4

Am anticipating the school holidays and a full ten days without the children. As I have three essays to write and two exams to sit for, I'm sure I will not be at a loss without them, but even so, after having had them as part of the daily reality for eight years, the idea of being without them is both a relief and a loss. Such an ambivalent position to be in once you have the children and have arranged your life around them. I can understand that women who know intellectually that they would be 'better off' without kids can still go ahead and have them or still keep them even when there is a chance to be without them. If there is no meaning to your life in its own terms, then kids can provide it – temporarily – and I guess some people opt for that rather than nothing. A difficult question but not one which will concern me after I have waved them good-bye. I have a sneaking suspicion that I will feel 'liberated' rather than 'lost' when they have gone. I might even be able to get more than 5 hours sleep a night.

Item 5

It seems that my role in this letter has become that of the pessimistic oracle. You mentioned in your last communication the value of humour and that we should have much more of it. I agree – but I think that we are deluding ourselves if we see it as a way to 'solve' anything. Seems to me that humour frequently gets used to divert attention from solving the real issues and instead acts as a sort of temporary relief valve to make it easier for us to go back to coping and to invisibility. It makes our lives easier for a moment but works against change. I have seen so many women who live with and deal with incompetent and stupid men, laughing off their foibles simply so that they can bear going home with them. It sort of saves face if you can pretend his stupidity and ignorance are really quite amusing and don't actually worry you. Laugh at him, laugh at yourself and prove to yourself and the world that it is all OK. Much more productive in the long term to get angry (conform to the humourless, feminist role) but unfortunately we may starve while we do it. There is no man who is going to pay for a woman to be mean to him – even if she does explain it's for the good of the next generation. I don't think very many men have been encouraged to see the needs and interests of the next generation as more important than their own needs and interests. We wouldn't have a concept of war, if that were the case. It really is rather silly to pretend that you are fighting a war for the sake of the next generation while at the same time you send the majority of them out to be killed. It is more sensible, I think, to explain war in terms of the old and wise ones sending out the young ones in order that the interests of the wise and elderly will be preserved – at whatever cost. And, of course, recorded in the halls of learning.

So, full circle and back to the halls of learning. The children have just reminded me that it is past their bed-time and that I promised them another chapter of Judy Blume's *Superfudge*. They love her books – and her sense of humour. I thoroughly enjoy them myself but wish they were slightly less 'traditional' in the portrayal of parents. Tell you what – you write your fiction while on holidays and I'll write some 'humorous' kids stories. We'll see what we come up with!

P.S. Re the facilities for disposal of 'sanitary' items in public conveniences. I noticed the other day that many here are provided by Rent-o-kil – the pest eradicators. Do you think that is significant?

If there is one thing that can be said for the young it is that they can so easily make us feel old! We had a collective meeting for the journal here on Thursday and afterwards went out for coffee – plus food (there being but coffee here and some of my sisters being ravenous). We had had a fairly intense discussion about how to save the world and although I can't say that I was directly involved there were occasions when particular feminist arguments seemed to assume life and death proportions, so a 'breath of fresh air' was quite welcome. As we walked down the King's Road it was not possible to remain oblivious to some of the younger members of our fair sex whose punk adornment is less than subtle, and I wondered what they would have made of our morning's discussion – for after all, we had been talking about *every* woman's experience.

So I decided to ask some of them.

First of all I had to convince them I wasn't a social worker, and then that I wasn't from some magazine. (Evidently they had answered some questions in the street once before from a person who purported to be a journalist . . . afterwards they had received some rather unwelcome material through the post.) I told them I was a writer . . . hardly sensible under the circumstances . . . they wanted to know for what magazine. It took some time to persuade them (understandably) I was just interested in them and their opinions, and I did get round to asking them what they thought about the women's movement. I got an earful. Serves me right.

When I realised I wasn't going to hear anything about the women's movement that could be remotely helpful, (it's just full of old bags, did you know?), I switched my questions to them and their lives. I didn't know whether to end up laughing or crying but I can honestly say that our efforts of the last decade haven't done much to change anything for the younger generation. (Of course my representative sampling techniques weren't all that good. There's bound to be a methodological argument somewhere against choosing the three most approachable looking young women in the King's Road on a Thursday afternoon ... early closing probably ruins the statistical validity. But I haven't the courage to try again.)

They were all 17 and one of them was supposedly at school and the other two left last year. What did they need qualifications for? Didn't I know there weren't any jobs? And walking up and down the King's Road (and by implication, finding someone who was prepared to buy you coffee and sitting time) was much better than being locked up in a stupid school. Anyway they didn't teach you anything there did they? I thought of Jay and concurred.

And boys? Well, heterosexuality wins, OK? (My words, not theirs.) Boys are what it is all about. Boys are why you come to the King's Road anyway. Boys are the reason for getting up in the morning, for getting dressed, and for coming to the King's Road and walking up and down. And who am I to be critical? Without boys there would probably be no reason to get out of bed. Looking for boys (I don't think they did much 'catching') was the sole source of their morale. I don't think they would see themselves existing if you took the boys away. So much for the feminist morning arguments about the delights of separatism.

We managed to talk about all manner of things but what did surprise me was their reticence on the topic of contraception. It seemed almost taboo. They talked freely – although not very personally – about sex, but I suspect none of them uses any form of contraception, and yet they led me to believe that boys automatically mean sex. Without being too prying I tried to ask them whether they had ever thought about pregnancy – and they assured me that they had not! Yet while they had me laughing I was feeling pretty dreadful inside. What does life hold for them? Are they heading for abortions or single parenthood at eighteen? I took your point about women laughing away the most awful problems.

I learnt something else as well while I was with them. I learnt that when you are young, dressed in bright colours and your hair sticks out at odd angles, you are not exactly made welcome in King's Road coffee places. The waiter made sure I could pay before he served us, we were watched the whole time we were there, and more than once I thought we were going to be asked to leave. That hasn't happened to me for ages – to think I am being allowed to stay in a place under sufferance. It was a good reminder of what it feels like to be something of an outcast. The girls told me they often get moved on – particularly when their plans are to make one cup of coffee 'do' for an hour. And where else can they go? Just walking up and down the street. That's their daily existence.

So when you write about some of the younger women you have met I can share some of the frustration. But I do wish I could work out how I feel about young women who have been educated, who do have jobs, and who defer in docile terms to their young men. There is no way I could blame my young friends for not doing something more constructive with their lives. They have so few resources. The entire world is against them it seems to me. But I do tend to want to shake young women who have so many more resources, who 'give them away' and still do nothing constructive with their lives. Except for the fact that it has overtones of Victorian morality (and the Lord helps those who help themselves), I think there are times when with some young women I feel more like shouting than sympathising. (Dad used to tell me I didn't know when I was well off when I used to complain about the way girls were treated, and it has rather ruined that phrase for me . . . but I have to admit that I understand the sentiment on occasion. Which could just mean that I am getting old as well.)

What does life mean to these young unemployed women? I

don't know. Does it have to mean anything? They didn't seem to look as though they were searching for meaning. It all seemed fairly straightforward to them, although they told me there were quite a few things they would like to see changed. They wanted more money for a start (a definite priority) and they wanted their mums to leave them alone. They had some bitter things to say about their mums who were always at them to do the housework, and to at least 'make themselves useful' if they couldn't bring in any money. One was very resentful about her older brother (also unemployed) who didn't have to help around the house and who got hand outs from her mum cause 'it's different for boys, they have to have more money'.

They seemed to have no ideas about the future – or none that they were going to tell me about. They were just living from day to day in the King's Road, and I suppose that's a fairly sensible approach considering that the future seems to have so little to offer them. They had no intention of trying to get on any youth training schemes, and no intention of looking for work, on the eminently logical grounds that both would be a waste of time. But even if they didn't want to talk about the future – and even though they were vehement in their dislike for housework, and for kids – I can't see that their lives will lead anywhere else except to housework and kids, and probably not in that order. It all seems so futile somehow.

From what you hear in the media you could be forgiven for thinking that it was only males who are unemployed – and who have problems. Back to the old pattern of male problems becoming *the* social problems. It's the boys that the establishment worries about – it's boys they are thinking of when they talk about 'alienation', about increases in anti-social behaviour, vandalism, drinking, crime rates and the ultimate breakdown in law and order. But what about the girls? They have just as many problems but because they don't cause as much trouble they can be ignored. Most of the statistics I have seen indicate that unemployment has risen more sharply among females than males and if the trend continues I suppose we will soon find ourselves back in the nineteenth century – with all the men in the work place and women in the home. Unemployed boys will be on youth training schemes and unemployed girls will slip quietly into being another pair of hands (albeit unwilling ones) to help with the unpaid housework. A bleak scenario but not beyond the realms of possibility.

But I have to admit that my young acquaintances didn't act as though the future was bleak. I thought they seemed to be enjoying themselves. They didn't miss a passing male (under about twenty I should think), they were quick to sum up the 'basics' crudely and concisely, and put paid to the idea that only girls are sex objects. Is it my middle class values coming to the fore or is it that there is more to life than this? Perhaps I am being very superficial in thinking that they were happy. Maybe what I was seeing was bravado – or desperation. Maybe when they aren't in the King's Road it all looks very different.

How could the women's movement relate to their lives? Or should it? There was nothing I could say to them. I felt completely inadequate. I can even appreciate the wisdom of the words of one 'friend' who also tells me that I don't live in the real world; if real is synonymous with lack of resources I know what he means.

The three young women had never met a women's libber and they were quite content for it to remain that way. (Two of them had had a teacher once who might have been – she was crazy enough, they told me.) It was all predictable stuff – women's libbers were old bags who couldn't get boys. I didn't try to change their minds despite the fact that their description of women's libbers was perilously close to that of the dreaded witches of former times.

So I am back with my uncertainties again and I am well aware that with the soul searching you are doing in trying to find a sensible explanation for the fact that you are doing law – you are not the best person to turn to for advice. I could send you a cable:

REQUEST MEANING OF LIFE REPLY POSTAGE PAID. Could you oblige?

Perhaps you do have the answer and there is something to be said for progeny after all – not only do they ensure that you get out of bed of a morning but they keep you so busy that you don't have time to ponder on the purpose of existence. Even if that is the case – it still doesn't seem a sufficiently sound reason for having them by the way.

I have been trying to think of what I would do if I was in charge of the world (after having sought your counsel of course). It's frightening to realise that you don't know and that no matter what plan you follow a huge proportion of the population would be upset. Take from the rich and give to the poor? Whether your hero is Jesus Christ, Robin Hood or Gough Whitlam it doesn't seem to be a plan exactly destined for success.

I don't even know if I could think of a suitable form of education. (This proves to be embarrassing when I am confronted with questions about what I would do to improve the system. It is not seen as modesty or humility when I say I don't know.) Have you any recommendations?

I have the deepest admiration for women who have written Utopian fiction. How did Charlotte Perkins Gilman envisage and detail 'Herland'? It seems so plausible and so possible the way she has portrayed it. No mother and daughter rifts, no fights over housework or childcare, no alienation and no injustice. I can't begin to create such a society, no matter how I tax my imagination. Every time I begin to think what it could be like, one of my friends creeps into my consciousness and displays characteristics which make it perfectly obvious that she wouldn't fit into my world scheme. If I turn to fiction I am sure it won't be utopian fiction that I write . . . it is too hard.

Roll on holiday. Reading and writing might be the signs of decadence in an unjust world but they are all I have. At least they don't make less sense than boys do to my three young King's Road women. Am I unduly depressed or is the present state of society an indictment of human imagination and will? I'd like to argue it would be better if we had women in power . . . but we have. So I think you and I should just keep our eyes open for a nice little deserted tropical island . . . and withdraw from the world. Maybe if it becomes a mass movement there'd be a labour shortage.

I have been trying to think of a witty response to your request for the meaning of life but am afraid that I have failed dismally. It's a trap to try and attribute the meaning of one's life to someone else – to family or relationships – because they are so unpredictable. Imagine if you tried to explain it in terms of children! Yesterday I had to arrange with Sue that she do child-care until 6.00 p.m. (while I was at one lot of lectures) and then hand over to the 15-year-old babysitter until I returned at 9.30 from another lot of lectures. I arrived home to find children still up, in (ragged) street clothes, very dirty and with food from one end of the bedroom(?) to the other. Every possible ingredient to turn a nice, orderly, middle-class mum into a raving lunatic. Jay and Aaron, who between them haven't as many years as the babysitter, had totally intimidated her. Fortunately, I was too tired to perform – too many essays, exams and late nights – so paid the sitter her money (equivalent to 4 packets of cigarettes or a good bottle of wine) and set about establishing some order. I did not kiss the children good-night nor read them a story. Next Friday, if Graeme is not available for child-care, I shall put them on the mini-bus to Wollongong and send them to mother. I will not even be concerned about the provision of a sickie-bag or instructions to Jay on how to collect and dispose of the results of Aaron's bus-sickness.

Surely such incidents cannot have anything to do with the meaning of life!

Part of the fatigue – then and now – is undoubtedly associated not just with the time it takes to do Law but the waste of time it represents in terms of the rest of my understandings about life. One of the basic premises of law is the 'on the other hand' concept whereby there are always at least two ways of approaching any problem – criminal or civil. However, while this could be seen as evidence of a moral understanding that people and events can be construed in different ways, this is not the case in Law. Instead, it is a game where no-one can catch out anyone else as 'wrong' because they have already admitted the possibility that there might be another way of looking both at the law and the facts. Further, it provides us with the (dubious) benefits of the adversary system whereby 'justice' emerges from whoever manages to fight best (dirtiest) in and out of the courtroom. A justice system based on such a premise can only have survived by keeping its practitioners far removed from accountability to the public . . . and this is what I'm working so hard to join?

I told you I had no answer to the meaning of life. The best I can do is come up with what is *not* the meaning of life.

Perhaps there is only what you construct and your young women in the King's Road are no better or worse off than the rest of us. Our sense of waste and our understandings about positive self-image may just be something that we've made up to justify our own efforts. Do you think it possible that some people might, just perhaps, feel good about having to deal with life only on a day-to-day basis? I think that denies our 'humanity'.

That's quite enough philosophy for one short session tucked in between kids, law, women's studies, house and writing – to say nothing of reading which last night produced your article as it appeared in the newspaper here. I knew it was due to come out but was aware that it somehow didn't quite seem the same as it was in the original you sent me. I checked one with the other and guess what? Every authoritative comment that you made had been changed into your 'personal' research and your 'personal' opinion. Thus your original, clear statement . . . 'Men are . . .' 'Dale Spender claims that men are . . .' and your use of negative male image in '. . . males are very emotion-al . . .' has been turned into a neutral comment about 'male emotion'. Clever, eh? Seems that it is your credibility that is being challenged and not that of the men whose behaviour you expose as being silly and predictable. The second and third last paragraphs of your original article in which you humorously mocked men, were left out altogether as was the part in the last paragraph where you suggested some strategies for what women might *do* about the problem of men talking too much. Do you think that there is a lesson in there somewhere . . . about the meaning of life, perhaps!

Talking of becoming emotional, I think you'd be most vulnerable at the moment in Australia. The jasmine that has always been part of mum's garden and now adorns my back fence, is in full bloom. I have discovered that if I put a vase of it in the study, the foul, stale, smoky smell is considerably cut down – or overpowered by the sweet pungent smell of the jasmine which is infinitely preferable. The whole garden is starting to blossom (literally) and I may even have true live tomatoes on the vine for you to pick next time you come to Australia. Why is it, by the way, that the spring-growth time of the year always reminds me of your birthday in September . . . warm weather, longer days, colourful gardens? And, more pertinently, why does my birthday always conjure images of coldness, darkness and not a flower to be seen? July 1st. Not only the middle of winter, but the beginning of the financial year. What hope have I got? I suppose if I were wealthy and lived in England, I'd think of July as 'rich', warm and colourful and of September as heralding the winter. There you see. That just goes to show that people who have travelled (with their minds open) have broader understandings and a greater sense of tolerance of differences. No wonder itinerant feminists are the most intelligent people I know!

I have managed this week to have a quick read of Bob Hawke's biography and commented to an obvious admirer of the man that I thought it not a great deal more than a 'boobs and booze' story (which is probably a little unfair because I have a great deal of respect for Blanche D'Alpuget who wrote it

– must have been the material and not the biographer). I was quickly reprimanded for being critical of an 'honest' portrayal and I think there was an element of respect being conveyed because he had agreed to expose such unpleasant aspects of his life. My own opinion is that the average Australian male (and let's face it Bob Hawke is pretty average) has no concept that his attitudes or behaviour in the 'boobs and booze' departments are unpleasant. In fact, I think most of them are rather proud if they can boast (with or without substantiation) of their conquests in either field of endeavour. Perhaps though I just do not move in the right circles. Perhaps somewhere in Australia (it certainly doesn't seem to be at the University, in law, politics, in engineering or in schools) there are hundreds of sensitive, intelligent well-informed men who read Virginia Woolf, who are aware of their inadequacies and who are appropriately humble about them – occasionally at least. Not that occasional humility makes that much difference overall. Canadian men were so much more humble than Australian men . . . that is, they treated women with exactly the same disregard but were aware when their treatment met with disapproval and were prepared to apologize before they did the same things again. Ultimately, you know, you can reduce men to manners. All that distinguishes one man from the other is the relative degree of sophistication that each reveals as he sets about getting his own way. Shame really. They could have so much potential as human beings if they weren't such a dull and homogeneous group!

'Aha' they say. 'Look how bitter, twisted and humourless feminists are!'

You know I have been interviewing young women here about marriage (for the methodology part of an assignment where I argued that young women within a 1 mile radius of my home were a more respresentative sample for me to deal with than names extracted from the electoral roll). They are a bit different from the King's Road women and I wonder how much is attributable to:

(a) the weather differences

(b) their 'social' (or in jargon – socioeconomic) status
(c) their level of education
(d) the circumstances in which I 'interviewed' them.

As far as (a) is concerned, there is no doubt that it is easier to live here on minimal amounts of money, (the dole), purely and simply because its not as cold and basic food is not as expensive as in London. Thus perhaps aspirations are different – the hopelessness of it all is not as apparent. For (b) – those women at uni whom I asked about marriage, with the exception of one who stated loudly and clearly that she would never marry, all saw it as an option in the future but one which had to wait until they were ready. Most of these women, not surprisingly, were from middle-class sorts of families with a sense of being able to influence the environment in some way. The others who were just 'working until they found a bloke' saw marriage as what life was all about. No consideration at all to statistics about marriage breakdown nor even to the fact that for several of them, their parents had separated and divorced under awful circumstances. A real sense of 'it will be different for me' . . . 'I wouldn't marry a man like that . . .' None of these had any college education but I don't think it's the education that makes the difference. Staying on at school is more a reflection of options than of a desire to learn more or understand more about those options. Seems to me that the young women who were preparing themselves to accommodate a man and marriage are in a fairly similar situation to your King's Roaders. What do you think?

As for (d) – always have to consider that when you are formally interviewing someone they might either give you what you want to hear and what they think they *should* be saying or that they will do just the opposite and over-exaggerate what you don't expect to hear. Sort of a performance . . . I have an idea that the university women were a bit inclined to say the 'right' things and the others delighted in saying the 'wrong' things. I think I'd be tempted to be a bit outrageous if some woman came asking me personal questions!

I finally had to conclude that women, as they have for

centuries, fairly realistically assess the options available to them – even when that means that marriage is the only feasible way of changing anything in your life – and take advantage of them as they are best able. You know I started off saying what a hoax marriage was and how women were tricked into providing free services for men. I still think that at one level, but am also aware that marriage provides a way for many people – the *only* way – to reassure themselves that they are alive and have some value. If that means that they have to marry to survive – psychologically as well as economically, then I can only encourage them to marry and hope that the sooner they do, the sooner they will learn that such is not what life is all about. Maybe they'll be motivated to change and reorganize. Talk about Utopian fiction. All this assumes that men have no say in the matter and that society does not work directly against women who feel the need to change and assert themselves in some way. And I know damn well that men and society do ulti-mately work against women. They have to or the whole basis of social organization would fall apart. Back to bombs, I suppose.

Meanwhile, I am exorcising my own demons as I write my book about marriage . . . it has been a long time in the writing hasn't it? And for good reasons. The more I think about it and explore it, the more dimensions I find and the less I can generalize about it. I guess I'll just have to do as you recommend and choose my particular 'audience' and write for her. I have by-passed you this time as I don't think you're quite the right person to approach . . . you already understand far too much about me, marriage and men.

Must turn my thoughts to mundane things and make a shopping list – including new shoes for the kids. I think they eat their shoes, although one turned up the other day which had been lost for months. It was in the ceiling where it had been 'turfed' through the manhole. (What do you think by the way of that term . . .? It distresses me every time I lie in the bath and realize that there is a 'manhole' above my head. Aware as I am of the male tendency to voyeurism, I rarely spend a long, relaxed time in the bath. Besides, I could always have a shoe fall on my head whilst I lie there!)

✁ Three Years Later

Scribbling Sisters was not immediately seized upon by a publisher: on the contrary it was (scathingly) rejected by many of the best known publishing houses in Australia and England. By April 1983 we had almost decided to call it a day and to save on further postage (and to save our psyches from further rejection) by filing our manuscript under the heading – 'Unpublishable'.

Then Sylvia Hale (of Hale and Iremonger) restored our spirits when she told us she *did* want to publish *Scribbling Sisters*, and when she assured us that our letters were 'a wonderful read'. She showed such good judgement of course, that it was a pleasure to work with her and in October 1984, *Scribbling Sisters* was published in Australia.

The only problem was that we were forced to take back some of our words about irresponsible reviewers: with a few exceptions we received such positive and constructive reviews that we were able to shrug off some of the devastatingly dastardly dismissals that we had initially received from publishers and their readers.

Fortunately, Sian Williams of Camden Press shared Sylvia Hale's enthusiasm for *Scribbling Sisters* with the result that the book will now be available outside Australia. Which will gratify our good friend Susan Koppelman in the United States; we had sent her a copy of *Scribbling Sisters* and she wrote a wonderful review of it in which she urged her fellow Americans to demand its appearance in their local bookstores. And she was most distressed when her review – was rejected.

Dear Lou,

'We do not ordinarily publish people's letters until after their death.'

That has to be one of the least helpful comments among all the rejection letters I have in front of me. Should we have written back and thanked them for their words of wisdom and added that though ordinarily disposed to follow publishers' advice this was one recommendation that we felt unable to accept? (Perhaps they were just politely telling us to 'drop dead'; I hadn't thought of that before!)

To be more serious, I don't think I could have faced all these readers' reports and rejection slips *en masse*, if I didn't know that the book *had* been published. I don't even feel vindicated (a good feminist word) when I read some of the statements . . . like 'there is no market for such material' and that our letters are nothing other than 'a dry husk of banal ideas' (I quote directly). But I do get distressed that 'readers' can feel it appropriate to make such savage comments and I do wonder just how many 'unpublished writers' there are who have had to contend with this type of 'hate mail'. It seems rather unjust that one should go to the trouble of writing, xeroxing, packaging and posting, only to get poison pen letters in return. For that's what some of the anonymous readers' reports really are.

(I wonder what sort of letters James Joyce got: all I

have in his quote above my desk is the entry from his own letters;

'Ten years of my life have been consumed in correspondence and litigation about my book, *Dubliners*: it was rejected by 40 publishers, three times set up and once burnt. It cost me about 3,000 francs in postage, fees, train and boat fare, for I was in correspondence with 110 newspapers, 7 solicitors, 3 societies, 40 publishers and seven men of letters about it. All refused to aid me, except Ezra Pound. In the end it was published, and in 1914, word for word as I wrote it in 1905. My novel [*Portrait of the Artist as a Young Man*] was refused by every publisher in London to whom it was offered – refused [as Mr Pound informed me] with offensive comments. When a review did decide to publish it, it was impossible to find in the United Kingdom a printer to print it.'

Clearly we were fortunate!

But this certainly raises the issue that no two people arrive at the same view of the world from the same physical evidence. I have been doing a cut and paste job with our rejection slips and reviews, sorting them into pros and cons, and the only logical conclusion that I can reach is that these people read different manuscripts.

'Represents the worst kind of male thinking and writing, rigid and impersonal and taking itself too seriously' (Australian publisher), alongside 'Dale's letters are wonderfully inventive, witty monologues . . . and Lynne comes across in her letters as equally ironic, and equally inventively clever in both her critique and the imaginative variety of her suggested solutions' (Susan Nicholls, *Sydney Morning Herald*, 5th January 1985). Now perhaps both assessments *are* a bit excessive (I am sure that what Susan Nicholls calls wit and irony, dad would call quite something else) but when you have two such diametrically opposed evaluations you are obliged to ask whether both readers read the same book.

(More to the point, what does this mean for marking and grading in education? I have always been critical of examinations and have suspected that one reason little or no research has been done on the validity of essay marking is because it would soon emerge that the same essay could get anything from 0% to 100% depending on who marked it. Obviously manuscripts can get anything from zero to 100% depending on who 'marks' them.)

I know we risk being cynical when we give other writers advice about publishing . . . 'It's not what you write but who you know' . . . but how else can we explain this continuum from venom to veneration? And I am almost astonished (note the qualification) by the internal contradictions. I know Karl Marx insisted that there was much to be said in favour of the inherent contradiction, but even he, I think, would object to some of these 'liberties'.

Have you noticed in the correspondence of one Australian publisher (who shall remain nameless . . . but the one that sent the *biggest* package of condemnatory criticisms, so you know who I mean), have you noticed that it says (a) that you can tell these are letters because they are ungrammatical and have an unfinished quality but (b) they will therefore have to be heavily edited and the sentence structure tidied up . . . presumably so you can't tell that they are letters! And on the same page in which our 'information' is condemned – I tell no lies – it also says 'Their style is stiff, formal and public'. Is schizophrenia a qualification for writing a reader's report I wonder?

Do I sound carping? I don't mean to. In fact there's part of me that is quite gleeful about receiving all this data for research. We couldn't have organised a better experiment even if we had tried. But just the same, I did find some of the comments very hurtful. They actually stopped me writing for days. And if I didn't have you to write to about this, if I kept it all bottled up inside, I am sure that the result could be paralysing. (Obviously no bad thing as far as some of these readers are concerned.) But do the women who write these reports know what power they wield when they forward their damning comments to writers?

I know it isn't necessary to write such destructive reports. I've edited a journal, edited books, and even been a publisher's reader myself on more than one occasion, and I'd be prepared to put $100 in Jay's bank account each time if ever I wrote rejection letters which were anything like the ones we received. I've never yet read anything that has nothing in it worth praising, and I always try and suggest ways of strengthening a manuscript. Which takes longer, I know, than straightforward denunciations. (Sorry about that sentence construction; will it get edited out?)

Have any of these readers ever been on the receiving end do you think? (Perhaps we should try another 'experiment'!)

Doing '*For the Record*'* really brought home to me just how damaging such comments can be. When I sent Phyllis Chesler and Robin Morgan the chapters I had written on them – and asked them had they been fairly represented and informed them that I would publish any comments they cared to make – I wasn't prepared for their responses. It hadn't really hit me just how much women writers had been hurt by the scathing dismissals of their work, and their persons. I thought they were two very successful writers who would graciously reply, but they are also two more women who have been crushed at times by destructive criticism. They were more saddened than embittered but it was salutary to get their replies and to realise that they too have been delivered body blows from which they have taken a long time to recover. And I am not sure whether they have completely convinced themselves that it is worth the risk of writing again.

I know when I got the reports on '*Reflecting Men*'† it took me days to get over it. Every time I sat down at my desk, solitary and quiet, the only thing that came flooding into my head were some of those comments that had leapt from the page . . . 'dull, boring, a paucity of ideas'. It's not the sort of stimulus that inspires you to take up your pen. And when I did put pen to paper I had to check everything against those criteria; was it

---

* '*For the Record; The Making and Meaning of Feminist Knowledge*', published by the Women's Press, London, 1985.
† '*Reflecting Men*', by Sally Cline and Dale Spender, forthcoming (hopefully) from André Deutsch in 1986.

dull, boring and lacking in ideas, I kept asking myself? And most of the time I thought it was . . .

A lot of writing is about confidence. It's about taking risks, exposing yourself and making yourself vulnerable. And if the confidence goes, the writing dries up. And it surely does go when branded into your brain are the words 'stupid and sterile'. How do you get the confidence back, and take the risks again? The goddess knows, I am no masochist. (By the way did you note that report that said 'irritating use of Christess and Goddess: why replace a cliché with a feminist interpretation of it?' Should we send an answer . . . 'Sadly life is a cliché – and we are trying to replace it with a feminist interpretation'? Or will we be misinterpreted?)

Anyway sister mine, if I keep on with all these sobering thoughts I will soon be depressed. Can't help having a giggle though about – 'I don't think it will be possible to market this to the male population. Most references to males are pretty scathing . . . I would perhaps edit some of the more heavy-handed anti-male comments' (Australian publisher's reader's report). Us! Anti-male? How preposterous! And what does she mean that it won't be possible to market the book to the male population? Doesn't she know the *Bookseller*'s figures that show it is women, not men, who buy books anyway? Publishers who try and market books for men that are neither about sport nor titillation seem to go broke. (Does that count as a heavy-handed anti-male comment?)

You know, one of the nicest things to emerge from all this is the number of comments that I have had from women who have read '*Scribbling Sisters*' and who have told me that they have resolved to take up letter writing again . . . not as a chore but as a pleasure. That we write to each other so often (and that our letters *were* published and validated – before our death) has helped to re-establish letter writing as a means of self analysis and development, and communication. (I don't want to claim too much for our venture of course, but letter writing has been 'a woman's art' for centuries and it has been virtually invisible. It's rewarding to see it as a 'topic', and it's one of the reasons that I want to do the history of women's letter writing.)

I met two wonderful Australian women at the University Women's Club. Di and Robyn. They have joined our monthly dining club.* You'd certainly think that on the nights that we meet there that the feminist take-over had already occurred. All these 'younger' women enjoying themselves. Makes quite a change from the usual quiet and refined atmosphere when there are twenty happy feminists in the dining room. And both Di and Robyn were saying that they had read 'Scribbling Sisters' in Australia, before they left, and that afterwards they were completely determined to keep in touch with their own sisters by letter when they came over here. Like you and me they hadn't found it hard to write regularly. It gets to be a bit like eating when it becomes part of your routine, doesn't it? You feel something's missing if you go a few days without food and you feel something's missing if you go a few days without letter writing.

I was explaining some of my theories about 'letter writing' to Di and Robyn – I think they were a bit taken aback to find that what they had accepted as an 'innocent pastime' I had elevated to the level of 'lit-crit theory'. But I'd just handed in 'Mothers of the Novel; 106 Good Women Writers before Jane Austen'† and I suppose I was still a bit high on finishing it, and ready to talk. I told them about women being the originators of the novel – that when women were allowed no education or public office they had still been permitted letter writing. And that it was a cunning move on women's part to start expanding the genre of letter writing to tell stories and to explain moral precepts (isn't that what we do in our letters to each other most of the time?). It's not coincidence that the first novels were epistolary novels – and written by women. And read by women!

Got close to giving an after dinner speech on the letter as literary form – and women's province. Suppose I should shut

---

* The University Women's Club has a mature and sedate membership and one purpose of starting the dining club was to introduce younger (feminist) women to the club and to seek their support . . . which does amount to a feminist take over.

† Forthcoming from Routledge & Kegan Paul.

up about it though. Otherwise men will latch on to it – and be seen to do it so much better. That's what happened with the novel. All those fantastic women writers who established the form and then along came a few men who appropriated it, and who were not only held to be better at it, but were given the credit for inventing it. It takes a man to do it properly! (Another anti-male comment . . . or maybe this one will be misconstrued as praise!)

Now is this dull? Is it boring? Does it lack ideas? I suppose it does. Writing to you I have never really thought about the merits of the writing. I do take the point that what interests us might be of little interest to anyone else though. Still, it's advantageous to know now the reception to our letters. Wouldn't be much use to us to wait until we were dead.

More exciting is that I am trying to get myself sorted out for a trip home, courtesy of University of Alberta at Edmonton. So nice to be *wanted* by North American universities when (again) I am so summarily rejected in the land of my birth. You know, when the Humanities Research Centre at the Australian National University advertised for candidates for its 1986 session on 'Feminism in the Humanities' I did actually think I stood a good chance of a fellowship. Particularly since part of their brief is to bring home those who are working overseas. But again, while I get more requests than I could possibly fulfil to lecture in the USA, Canada, and Scandinavia . . . nothing from Australia. Why is that do you think? (I have just received a list of the people who were successful . . . mostly men, particularly those who qualified as Marxists.)

A lot of people over here did apply and many of them expected that I would be going. Quite embarrassing to explain that like them, I got a proforma rejection slip. And even more embarrassing to try and explain the criteria behind the selection of the successful candidates. Had to tell a few that I cannot be held accountable for the thinking of Australian selection committees.

Sour grapes? Maybe. But I do wonder *who* did the selecting. Some of the same people who wrote those readers reports?

I go to Alberta in September. And as it costs only £200 more to get back to London via Sydney, (I never can work out the principles behind air fares) you can expect me for three weeks in October. I should have earnt enough in Canada to satisfy Jay's capitalist cravings and to be able to pay enough piss-off money to procure for us a couple of days of peace and quiet. Although now that Aaron has taken to piano playing, I suppose the rates for silence have increased considerably.

The only cloud on my horizon is that you will sit there disapproving while I indulge in the occasional furtive cigarette. Unlike you, I have not been able to give up the filthy habit, although you have scared me sufficiently to cut down on them. But will you promise not to purse your lips and say 'It's your health you are harming' each time I light up?

The only other problem is what am I to do with Mrs Pepys when I take off for foreign parts? Do you think I should take her with me.* I don't know if I can bear to leave her, she has become so much part of my life. I abandoned her for two weeks when I went to the National Women's Studies Conference in America and I felt quite lost without her. It's hard to keep her in perspective and to remember that she is a 'character' of my own making . . . I should be the first to make quips about other people's mental state when I keep hearing voices myself . . . and in seventeenth-century English!

This afternoon's exercise is to go through Mr Nicholas Culpepper's '*Complete Herbal and English Physician*' published in 1653. You know about Mrs Pepys's period pain, and the abscess on her labia (poor woman!). Much speculation that the abscess was the result of syphillis, given her by Samuel. Well, I know all that; what I don't know is what she did for the abscess and the pain. Samuel records that she was ill – and that he got ointments for her, but not what they were. And I can't bear to think of her putting up with it all. So to Mr Culpepper . . . whose book would have been available at the time.

---

* Dale is currently writing '*Mrs Pepy's Diary*' for publication by Granada in 1987.

The marvellous Candida* bought me a reprint of Mr Culpepper's original book and I have been discovering cures for almost everything. (Nothing for AIDS I am afraid.) Already I have come across 'Golden Rod': it 'flowereth in the month of July' and can be used for a range of ailments.

'The decoction of the herb, either green or dry, or the distilled water thereof, is very effectual for inward bruises, likewise for staying the floodings of the body, as fluxes of humours, body fluxes, and the immoderate menses of women . . . It is a sovereign wound-herb whereby green wounds and old ulcers are speedily cured; it is of particular efficacy in all lotions for sores and ulcers in the mouth, throat or privities of either sex. A decoction is serviceable to fasten the teeth when loose.'

As Mrs Pepys had trouble with her teeth as well, I think 'Golden Rod' answers for just about everything. (Should I tell Jay? Maybe he could market it . . . it wouldn't be the MOST illegal way to make his fortune!)

So to Mrs Pepys and her female troubles this afternoon. Will send you the latest chapter when completed. Please do not provide reader's reports of the kind that currently litter my desk. Only ten weeks till I see you. Miss you.

---

* Candida Lacey works with Dale and looks after the post when Dale visits Lynne . . . a thankless task.

✦ Coogee, July 1985

Dear D,

Received your 'dry husk of rather banal ideas' this afternoon along with law results for this semester (now there's some genuine dry husks for you – the law, not the results), the July issue of Australian Book Review, a royalties cheque from RKP, a rates-overdue notice, a telephone bill and 2 glossy catalogues advertising heaters (it is winter here, you know). Unfortunately I had no chance to sit and pretend that I was a 'lady' by indulging in a leisurely reading of the mail. Jay came racing in the back door with the RED-ALERT look, followed by Aaron, shrieking that Charles from next door had been injured – probably killed. As it transpired Charles had indeed been injured – as a direct consequence of Aaron's dare-devil feats on his bicycle. Thus we had to deal not only with Charles's lacerated head (a trip to casualty at the local Children's Hospital) but also with Aaron's sense of self as he came to terms with the fact that he contributed to the injury. I am still not sure whether he has managed to draw the fine line between 'my fault' and 'accidents do happen', but he seems to be working it out without major trauma. Quite surprising really as Jay delights in standing over him saying things like 'You could have killed someone . . . you could be in jail . . .' and other brotherly delights.

I finally managed to open the mail after the children retired to bed. ('Have you showered? Have you shampooed? Have you cleaned your teeth? When did you last change those pyjamas? I don't know where your toothbrush is. It could not be in the washing basket unless you put it there. I don't know why Aaron's shoes are in the washing basket' . . . to mention just a few of the warm, rewarding and intimate exchanges between a mother and her children before they settle into bed for the evening). I was almost sorry that I did.

Who'd be a writer? The incoming cheque from RKP – royalties on 'Intruders' for a year – was £76; the outgoing bills totalled $300.00. Even with the Australian dollar at its highest and the pound at its lowest, the two hardly match up. On top of that, Australian Book Review carried an article about Sylvia Hale – the one Australian publisher to acknowledge (before publication) that 'Scribbling Sisters' might have some value. The article detailed the huge problems she faces as one of our few independent publishers – what little chance there is here to publish anything removed from the mainstream and still make enough money on it to help finance the next project. (You don't think 'Scribbling Sisters' might have contributed to the problems, do you?).

Then, as the last straw, comes your letter with the comments about publishing and readers' reports. Hate Mail!! Poison Pen Letters!! It was enough to make me think that we would have been better staying in the safe harbour of the NSW Education Department as English teachers. But you destroyed that one too. You point out that we would still have been caught up in the system of making arbitrary decisions about 'good' and 'bad' essays. Besides, you would probably have had us both sacked by now. I do remember the time you refused to give normal distribution curve marks to the English students and so mucked up the entire school system. You weren't all that popular, were you?

The only solution that I can offer for the problem of reviews and readers' reports is to change the entire publishing industry. As it is, everything works on supply and demand – basic economics. The idea is to limit the supply of books that are published in order to stimulate demand for them. Thus it is a far, far better (and easier) thing to do to reject a manuscript than to recommend it. By rejecting it, you are helping publishers to limit the supply. Besides, if you recommend a manuscript, you get caught up in all sorts of additional jobs and meetings where you have to prepare material and justify your opinion. If you reject it nothing more is ever heard of the matter and (if you're lucky) you still receive your reader's fee.

I'm sure that publishers prefer rejection reports – for similar reasons. Just think of all the work that publishers have to do if someone recommends a manuscript and it is accepted. It's a dreadful bother. There are budgets to do, costings, and all those nasty details of layout, typesetting, proofreading, as well as the hassles of marketing and distribution. And you have to pay something to those damned authors. Very much easier to use the income generated from established lists to pay selected readers to reject manuscripts. That way, the publisher can feel in control. The relatively few books that do get published assume enormous importance and the publisher can bask in the reflected glory – his importance can actually rise on the basis of how *few* books he publishes rather than on how *many*. I suggest that the publishing industry be restructured so that the basic reason for the existence of individual publishers is . . . wait for it . . . to publish as many books as they can!!! We could offer incentives for publishers who did the most/best books for the year (best being of course what people most liked). What a dangerous thing to do. It could be the end of the publishing industry . . .

Perhaps it would just be easier to insist that all reviewers and readers qualify as veteran letter-writers. If, as you say, letter writing encourages self analysis and awareness then it is only appropriate for those who pass judgement on others to be aware of their own motives. Good heavens! That sounds almost biblical. Must be time I took a break. Shall return to this later . . . (Later . . . two days)

Charles' head is on the way to healing; Aaron has totally erased any memory of his involvement in Charles's 'accident' and I am still cross, upset, disturbed – whatever – about the seemingly perennial problem of women and writing. The women you wrote about in *For The Record*. Why should they feel their whole identity is at stake when they write? Why should they (you? I?) feel as though we are perpetrating some sort of trick on the rest of the world? I guess it has something to do with calling yourself a writer. It is seen as a claim to be 'different' – and it seems, a challenge to all and sundry to try to prove that they (you, we) are very ordinary and even less bright/clever/witty etc. than the reader or reviewer who is commenting on the book.

It really is a cheap trick. Anyone can read a book, make a few nasty comments about it and get their name in the paper or get paid a reader's fee. More rewarding than spending a year (or three) writing the damned book only to get £76 and a case of identity crisis brought on by scathing reviews. I suppose I should develop some objectivity about the issue – stand back from it – view it philosophically as yet another example of how 'power' works in this world of ours. As an adult dealing with two relatively powerless children, and as a female in this oh-so-male Australian society, I am aware how easy it is not only to take advantage of being in the powerful position, but to justify it on all sorts of (spurious) grounds (i.e. disciplining the children 'for their own good'; rejecting manuscripts to keep up the 'standards' of Australian literature-Ha!; refusing to appoint a woman to the position because 'there just isn't one qualified for the job').

To more pleasant topics.

I had dinner on Wednesday night with Debra at her flat in Manly. Right on the beachfront and apart from the problems that we both have with the males who inhabit such areas after dark (they pee in her front entrance hall while they use our fence), it is a delightful spot. She had gone to a great deal of trouble and after several glasses of wine read me some of her 'novel'. It is clever. I would like to think I could claim some reward for her ability, but of course, I can't. She had the same thoughtfulness and independent approach even when she was 16 years old, at school. One of those students to earn the arbitrary 100% for her essays, even then.

My only complaint about the evening was aimed at her dog,

Oscar – a *he* who has developed all the traits that I have tried to prevent Jay 'n' Aaron from acquiring. Within two minutes of my arrival at the flat, Oscar had brought out all his toys and demanded that we deal with him. When he realized we were more interested in the food and conversation, he began dragging himself across the floor in front of us in quite flagrant exhibitions of dog-masturbation. There we were, two sensitive women, minding our own business, while this male-dog-child demanded our attention. We may just as well have been at an Australian pub.

Talking of dogs, we are still entertaining the one that mother and father so thoughtfully gave to the children for Christmas. They had some old-fashioned idea that it might develop a sense of responsibility in the children if they had to look after a puppy. Very funny. It may have developed my already over-burdened sense of moral righteousness but it has done bugger all for the children – and less than that for my back garden. Every time I walk out there to do the sorts of romantic things that one reads about in books, like picking fresh sprigs of parsley from my herb garden or plucking tropical flowers to decorate the dinner table, I find that 'Ms', the dog, has entertained herself by destroying yet another pot-plant. Apparently a great deal of pleasure can be derived from upending the pots, chewing the roots and scattering pieces of both from one end of the yard to the other. At least she is thorough.

I really don't know how to respond to the news of the fellowship at Australian National University. It's fairly empty-sounding to say that you were probably over-qualified and very tempting to say that the selection committee obviously had their own reasons for accepting Marxist males rather than feminist females. I mean, if you weren't a feminist and you had to decide, which would you prefer . . . six stroppy women or six dopey men? So much less trouble and absolutely no competition to have in a few dull men for a period of time. They probably set up the selection committee on the same basis as they choose reviewers for feminist books – anyone other than a feminist will do!!

And don't forget the Australian tall poppy syndrome. We don't like tall poppies here – someone even wrote a book about it last year. Instead of having your head chopped off when you step out of line, here we pull the rug out from underneath you. Especially if you had the audacity to 'make it' in another country. It's par for the course here. If you set yourself up in any way in the public world, you can expect that sooner or later someone will try to pull you down and will think themselves very clever for doing so. The world does move slowly. I remember the section in *'Intruders on the Rights of Men'* where women in the 1840s decided not to use their own names for published work – not only because readers would be prejudiced against women writers but because the consequences of 'going public' were so horrendous.

Even so, all is not lost! I did tell you about the letter that came from Thomas Nelson publishers (a female editor) congratulating us on *'Scribbling Sisters'* and saying that their rejection of the manuscript was one case of a publisher being wrong. Rather nice to read it after the barrage of criticism of our 'superficial ideas', our 'soap opera rhetoric' and our 'heavy-handed attempts to be funny'. As I said, who'd be a writer?

I must turn to being other things. Domestic chores are mounting up. It's time I hit the children with a new set of rules for bedroom, bathroom and kitchen cleaning – they get bored with the old ones after a while. Mother and father are due home from their trip some time next week and I should go and air the house and stock up on provisions before they arrive – as well as be there when they finally return. Lectures resume next week – and the work schedule is gaining momentum as the time approaches for me to have completed my paid job of editing *'The Law Handbook'*. It's supposed to be ready by October . . . At least I am not bored!

Managed three credits in the law exams, according to the official results,

Much love,

Lou

✕ Works referred to in the letters
(Place of publication London, unless otherwise stated.)

Mary Astell (1964), *A Serious Proposal to the Ladies*, reprinted in Katherine Rogers (ed.), *Before Their Time: Six Women Writers of the Eighteenth Century*, New York 1979.

Jessie Bernard, *The Future of Marriage*, New York 1972.

Gloria Bowles & Renate Duelli Klein (eds), *Theories of Women's Studies*, 1983

Eleanor Dark, many novels including, *Slow Dawning* (1932), *Prelude to Christopher* (1933), *Return to Coolami* (1935).

Matilda Joslyn Gage (1873), *Woman Church and State: The Original Expose of Male Collaboration Against the Female Sex*, reprinted Watertown, Mass. 1980.

Charlotte Perkins Gilman (1892). 'The Yellow Wall-paper', reprinted in Ann J Lane (ed.), *The Charlotte Perkins Gilman Reader*, 1981.

Charlotte Perkins Gilman (1915), *Herald*, reprinted 1980.

Philip Goldberg, 'Are Women Prejudiced Against Women?' (eds), *And Jill Came Tumbling After*, New York 1974.

Erica Jong, *Witches*, 1982.

Susan M Lloyd (ed.), *Roget's Thesaurus of English Words and Phrases*, 1982.

Drusilla Modjeska, *Exiles at Home: Australian Women Writers 1925–1945*, Melbourne 1981.

Adrienne Rich, *Of Lies, Secrets and Silence*, 1980.

Robyn Rowland, *Women Who Do – And Women Who Don't, Join the Women's Movement*, 1982.

Sophia, A Person of Quality (1739), *Woman Not Inferior to Man*, facsimile reprint, 1975.

Dale Spender (1980), *Man Made Language*, 2 edn, 1985.

Dale Spender (ed.), *Feminist Theorists: Three Centuries of Women's Intellectual Traditions*, 1982.

Dale Spender, *Invisible Women: The Schooling Scandal*, 1982.

Dale Spender, *Women of Ideas – And What Men Have Done To Them*, 1982.

Dale Spender, *There's Always Been A Women's Movement This Century*, 1983.

Dale Spender (ed.), *Time and Tide – Wait for No Man*, 1984.

Dale Spender, *For the Record: The Making and Meaning of Feminist Knowledge*, 1985.

Dale Spender, *Mothers of the Novel: 106 Good Women Writers Before Jane Austen*, provisionally titled *Women and Writing*, in press.

Lynne Spender, *Intruders on the Rights of Men: Women's Unpublished Heritage*, 1983.

Lynne Spender, *Not Made in Heaven*, forthcoming.

Rebecca West, *The Young Rebecca: Writings of Rebecca West 1911–1917*, Jane Marcus (ed.), 1982.

Virginia Woolf (1928), *A Room of One's Own*, reprinted Harmondsworth 1974.

Virginia Woolf (1929), 'Women and Fiction', reprinted in Leonard Woolf (ed.) *Collected Essays: Virginia Woolf*, Vol II, 1972.

Virginia Woolf (1938), *Three Guineas*, reprinted 1977.